Equinomics:
The Secret to Making Money with Your Horse Business

Lanier Cordell

Esprit de l'Equestre PUBLISHING

Cover & Interior Design
Designed by Lanier Cordell
Photo courtesy of IStockPhoto.com
Illustrations courtesy of Dover Pictorial Archive Series/Master Clips and Microsoft.com Clipart

This book is dedicated to:

Eddie Ray Federwisch,
Tim Raisbeck and Mark Raisbeck,
who really understand that good customer service
is the basis of good marketing

to
Lynn Thomas and Linda Myers,
who made me write it all down

and especially to

deSaix Tankersley Hill and Stephen Tankersley,
who got me into the horse business in the first place

CONTENTS

Introduction   ix

Chapter One: Building the Foundation   1

Chapter Two: Do You Have What It Takes?   5

    Yearly Cost of Supporting the Average Horse   6

Chapter Three: Determining Your Target Market   9

    The Market   10

    Focused Market Sub-Segment   11

    Where to Find Information   14

    Demographics 14

    Demographics and Your Primary Business Focus   16

    Equine Assisted Psychotherapy   17

    What Your Existing Customers Can Tell You   18

    The Competition   19

    Sizing Up Your Competition   20

    Vision: How You Want Others to See You   22

    Positioning Yourself for Maximum Impact   23

    Goals   24

    Liability and Risk   25

    Taxes, Permits & Licenses   26

Chapter Four: Pricing   29

    Deciding What to Charge   29

    Charging What You Are Worth   30

    Profit Margins   31

    The Business Plan   34

Chapter Five: Marketing   37

    The Purpose and Ethics of Marketing   37

    A Great Demonstration of Effective Marketing   38

    Identifying Your Product or Service   40

    Who Are Your Customers?   41

    Logic vs. Emotion - Which one do you appeal to?   42

    Benefit VS Feature   45

Chapter Six: Marketing Communications   47

    Communicating Effectively   48

    Copy Writing Formula for Success   48

    Call to Action   50

    Make It Easy   50

    Positives and Negatives   51

    Fonts   51

Colors   53

Pictures and Clipart   54

One Size Doesn't Fit All   54

Testimonials   55

Professional Titles and Designations   56

Testing Your Materials   56

Tracking   58

Chapter Seven: Advertising   **59**

The Medium   60

What to Do with a REALLY Small Budget   62

The Advertising Budget   62

Frequency   63

Rates   63

Copy Writing 65

Design   67

Ads in Reverse   68

Color and Ads   68

Ad Size   69

Camera-Ready   70

Ad Agencies   70

Chapter Eight: Advertising Options   **73**

Logos   73

Signs   74

Prize Lists   75

NAHA Placemats   75

Brochures   76

Brochure Copy Writing   78

Business Cards   79

Web sites   82

Newsletters   84

Billboards   86

Chapter Nine: Public Relations   **91**

Press Coverage   92

Press Releases   94

Sample Press Release   95

Feature Articles   96

Contributing Columns or Articles   97

Other Ways to Get Your Message Out   98

Communicating with Your Customers   99

Chapter Ten: The Marketing Plan   **101**

Your Starting Point   101

What You Want to Accomplish   102

The Target Market   102

How You Are Going To Reach Your Goal   102

Timing   103

Budget   103

How You Are Spending Your Budget   104

Measuring Your Results   104

Chapter Eleven: What to Do When Your Marketing Efforts Work 111

Eliminating Negatives   111

The More Information Trap   112

Winning Customers   114

Chapter Twelve: Building Customer Loyalty   117

Keys to Profitable Customer Service 118

Your Competition   119

The 80/20 Rule   119

Understanding Value   119

Agressively Seek Complaints   119

Respond   120

Communicate Effectively   120

Collaborate   121

Chapter Twelve and a Half: Still Waiting for Your Prince?   123

Appendix   i

Size and Composition of Your Potential Market   iii

The Size and Composition of Potential EAL Corporate Training Market   iv

The Size and Composition of Your Potential EAP Market   v

Sizing Up The Competition   vii

Vision: How You See Yourself   ix

GOALS: Where Is Your Business Headed? x

Identifying Your Product or Service   xi

Sample Customer Survey   xii

Determining Your Costs   xv

Determining Your Income   xvi

Determining Your Profit Margin   xvii

Identifying Your Audience   xviii

Benefits Your Business Offers Potential Clients   xix

The Three Reasons For Doing Business With YOU!   xx

Your Most Important Benefit and Where to Use It   xxi

Your Brochure Cover   xxii

Inside Your Brochure - Panel 1   xxiii

Inside Your Brochure - Panels 2 & 3   xxiv

You and Your Qualifications   xxv

Brochure Layout Guide Back   xxvi

Brochure Layout Guide Front   xxvii

Sample of 3 Single Panel Brochure Fronts   xxviii

Sample of 3 Single Panel Brochure Backs   xxix

Sample of a Three Panel (3 fold) Brochure Back   xxx

Sample of a Three Panel (3 fold) Brochure Front   xxxi

Sample Logos   xxxii

Sample Logos   xxxiii

Sample Logos   xxxiv

Essential Parts of a Good Print Ad   xxxv

Sample Trainer Ads   xxxvi

Sample EAP/EAL Ads   xxxvii

Ad Layout Sheet   xxxviii

Business Card Sample   xxxix

Sample Postcards   xl

Sample Web Site   xli

Billboard Layout Work Sheet   xlii

Sample Flyer   xliii

Sample Student Press Release Form   xliv

Sample Tracking Sheet   xlv

Marketing Plan Form   xlvi

Additional Resources   1

Statistical Resources 1

Trade, Breed and Discipline Associations 1

Horse Councils   1

Government Agencies 1

Others 1

For Equine Assisted Psychotherapists: 1

Business Management   1

Facility Planning   1

Public Relations Resources   1

Suggested Reading li

Liability and Risk Reduction Resources lii

Insurance   lii

Books   lii

State Laws Governing Horses, Horse and Facility Owners lii

Safety Issues liii

Risk Reduction Plans liii

Introduction

There is an old saying that states, "The best way to earn a small fortune in the horse industry is to start with a large one." Anyone who works in the horse industry can certainly identify with that claim. Each year thousands of people start up horse-related businesses, put in long hours of physically demanding work and reap little or no profits. Within a few years the constant lack of money despite lots of hard work turns a large number of horsemen into bank tellers or other such mainstream occupations, and depletes many a fortune.

But why is this the case? Why is the horse industry a notoriously low-profit, high–effort proposition? From what I have observed in the 25 years I have been around horse businesses the reason is very simple - most people who open horse businesses do so because they love horses, not business. They have little or no understanding of profit margin, pricing, or marketing. All they know is that they love working with horses and want to turn their passion into a business.

Unfortunately, the horse industry, probably more than any other industry, requires far more than skill and talent to succeed. Whether you are a riding instructor, trainer, farrier, veterinarian, massage therapist, school riding program director, equine assisted psychotherapist, breeder, appraiser or other equine service provider or ancillary business, the secret to succeeding and actually making a descent living is simple – learn and practice good business principles with marketing topping the list.

I love marketing. It is safe to say that I am as passionate about marketing as you are about horses. I think it is one of the most fascinating and rewarding ways to spend my time. Studying people and how they behave, how they take in information, store, and toss it back, why they react the way they do captivates me. I love using that information to help clients make money, and I love the fact that marketing incorporates persuasion, writing and art in many forms. I love it because these things interest me and because I am good at them. Or it could be that I am good at them because I love them. Whichever, most horse people aren't good at marketing and don't love it. That's okay. It's not a flaw; it is simply a fact.

As you go through this book you may find that I've ended sentences with prepositions, used second person and other such grammatical faux pas that drive English teachers nuts and can be very effective for marketing purposes. The truth is I didn't write this book for English teachers. I wrote it for people whose livelihoods rely on horses.

I don't ride. I don't own a horse. At this point, I don't even pay a bill for a horse. But I know every facet of the horse industry intimately. I have a daughter who was bitten by the horse bug at the age of two. By age five she was riding bare back at a gallop on any horse she could find. When she was 9 she started showing hunters. By age 10 she was training green horses. From that time on, she road 3 or more times a week on two or more horses a day, went to all the schooling and rated shows in the area. She and her horse went to college at Virginia Intermont where she got her degree in equine studies and rode on the Intermont Intercollegiate Horse Show Association Hunter Equitation team. She is now a trainer/instructor. My son rode western, particularly roping. He is a graduate of the Oklahoma Horseshoeing School and, even though his primary job is working on diesel truck engines, he has a few horses that he regularly shoes. His daughter, Haley, rides ponies; her aunt, my daughter, is her trainer. My daughter's husband started out riding hunters as a child because his mother rode them. He switched to Western, and taught, trained, and showed reining from about the age of 12 through college where he rode on the Iowa State IHSA reigning team. He doesn't ride much now because he is an equine veterinarian specializing in performance horses and doesn't have the time. I sit on the equine studies advisory board for Virginia Intermont College and am the horse "expert" on their board of trustees. I also helped form the Intercollegiate Dressage Association into a national organization and serve on their board as public relations and marketing officer. I am the past president of the Louisiana State University School of Veterinary Medicine's Friend's Association. And I am co-chair of zone seven of the Interscholastic Equestrian Association.

During the last 25 years, I spent countless hours ringside listening to lessons, asking tons of questions, and observing what horse professionals encounter on a daily basis. And, while I'd never pretend to be a horse professional, I know enough about the industry to understand the special needs and problems that face those who work in all of its many facets. I also know marketing.

My goal in writing this book is not to make you a marketing whiz but to help you do a better job of getting good results no matter how small your marketing budget is, and to keep you from making costly mistakes. You may never love marketing as much as I do, but you should become more comfortable and confident, and get better results. At the very least, you may learn enough to be able to make good decisions in hiring someone to do your marketing for you.

To that end, this book contains vital information in what I hope is an easy to understand and easy to use format. It provides the bare bones that you need to turn your passion for horses into a profitable, and enjoyable business, or to turn a struggling business around.

I am writing this book because I feel passionately about the importance of horse professionals to the future of horses. For thousands of years horses have served mankind carrying him into battle, to new lands, to fetch a doctor in an emergency, to bring good news and bad, to farm and on and on. Horses have played a major role in the shaping of this world and, for that, they deserve to be respected, cherished, and preserved. However, despite their myriad contributions to mankind, their future is not guaranteed. The sad fact is that human beings have long had a habit of preserving only those things that are useful to them.

At the start of the twentieth century, horses were a vital part of everyday life in this country. By the end of the 1920s, horses were no longer the major method of travel; cars were. It took a little longer for engines to replace the horse on farms, but not by much. At the start of the twenty-first century, carriage operators, horse racing, Amish communities and a few working ranches are the only ones who use horses for anything other than pleasure. So it is up to you, the people who work in every aspect of the horse industry, particularly the recreational areas to see to it that this industry remains strong and growing, one business at a time. Ultimately, your success is a success for all horses now and in the future. As horse professionals you are guardians of a sacred trust. It is up to each and every one of you to guard it well. The best way to do so is to build the strongest, most profitable horse business you can.

It is often said, "If you do what you love, you never work a day in your life." Here is hoping that the tools provided in these pages will allow you to make money with your horse business so that you never have to work a day in your life, and that there will always be horses to share their magic with our world.

Chapter One

Building the Foundation

W hat marketing is and what it involves depends a lot on who you are talking to. Talk to a person who works in a large company with a sales force, and chances are highly likely that the first thing that will pop into that person's mind is "sales." If the person you are speaking to doesn't have a sales force, chances are very good that the first thing that will pop into his mind at the word marketing is "advertising." They are both right - marketing does involve sales and it does involve advertising, however these are a small part of actual marketing.

Marketing includes everything from choosing, shaping, packaging, and presenting your business to selling and promoting it. Since everything you do in business should be done so that it will ultimately result in making money, every aspect of your business is part of your marketing. This is true even if you are a non-profit business. If the non-profit service you offer isn't valuable to someone, if it doesn't fill a need, you won't find anyone to clients to help and you won't get the funding you need. If you don't have the funding, you can't continue to provide a noble service, which won't matter because you won't have anyone interested in receiving your help because they don't need it. Even non-profits have to live by marketing principles if they are to succeed. Sales will definitely help you reach your moneymaking goal, as will an effective advertising campaign. However, neither one will do you a bit of good if you don't have a product or service that a particular group of people feel they need, and are willing to pay for. Nor will a sales force or advertising campaign work, if it isn't aimed directly at, and shaped for those people who are most likely to buy your goods or services.

Marketing is a science and an art. The "science" of marketing is comprised of the statistical information used to determine the number and profile of those people who are most likely to buy your goods or services. The Science of marketing is also comprised of psychology of human beings and what motivates them. The "art" of marketing is comprised of the artwork, design, fonts and colors used in ads and promotional materials, the copy writing, and sometimes even the placement of marketing information and its presentation. Some people are better at the science portion, while others are better at the art. The better you are at both, the better your results will be. Regardless of what your strongest marketing skills maybe, you cannot afford to ignore either aspect if you want to build a profitable horse business.

Building a business, any business is just like building a building. I know that it sounds cliché but clichés are usually great truths that have been repeated so often that they are familiar to everyone.

If you take the time with this phase, you end up with a strong business that will withstand even the roughest storms.

It is very true that building businesses is like building buildings, and the foundation is the best place to start the process. It is also the most time consuming. But, in the end, the time spent on laying the foundation - choosing the location, measuring it out, setting the forms and the base, and making sure that every step is done as perfectly as possible is time well spent. If you take the time with this phase, you end up with a strong business that will withstand even the roughest storms. If you hurry through the process in a slip-shod fashion, skip a step here and there; any time or money saved will end up costing you far more down the road. As any builder can tell you, if the foundation isn't right, the building won't be either. Without a good foundation, the building will fall under the pressure of even a minor set back or have to be knocked down and rebuilt - if you can afford it. Generally when a business collapses, there isn't the money available to start over.

This being the case it is wise to really invest the time in getting the foundation of your business as right as it can be from the very beginning. Determining the nature of your business, discovering costs, setting prices, determining your goals, and identifying who your customers are, are all important parts of a good, solid business foundation.

Whenever I begin a new client relationship, I start by reviewing the information you will find on the next few pages. The reason for this is simple; I am hired because a client wants to earn more money. I can't begin to tell them how to make more money until I know what sort of foundation there is to build a marketing program upon. I have to fully understand what I am selling, why it is of value, and to whom it is valuable before I can craft an effective marketing campaign.

If you are just starting out in business or even if you have been in business for decades, this is where you need to begin. It has been my experience that no matter how long a client has been in business, they always benefit from going back to the foundation. To use the building metaphor again, existing businesses are like existing houses; you shouldn't consider buying or repairing one until you have it thoroughly inspected, and repair any damage or weakness in the foundation. Think of the next few chapters as an inspection of your business foundation. You may get a clean bill of health, or you may find that, with a few minor repairs, your business will be on much stronger footing. You'll also find it far easier to get more customers interested in coming to you, and giving you their money when your business is at its best.

New business owners or old should not skip this part and jump to advertising and public relations in search of glamour or quick fixes. I can guarantee you that even the most brilliant advertising and public relations campaigns in the world won't do you a bit of good if you don't have a strong enough product to sell. The strength of any marketing program, be it for goods or services, begins here. While it may not be as sexy as advertising and public relations, it is ultimately more important to your overall marketing efforts.

Chapter Two

Do You Have What It Takes?

It is amazing to me that so many people who know first hand how much work horses require still decide to take the leap and make the horse industry their career. The amount of physical work and time required is enough to discourage me from attempting it. But even more amazing to me are the number of students each year who apply to college equine studies and equine science programs who have never even ridden a horse or mucked out a stall, but still have a goal of working with horses as a profession. The explanation for this may be that they are interested in these career paths specifically because they have no clue as to what they are getting into. They are looking for something to major in, and they've always liked horses so a career involving horses seems more interesting than English Lit. An equally surprising number of aspiring horse professionals are people who finally fulfill a life-long desire to learn to ride and, after a few lessons, decide to make their hobby their career.

While the first group of experienced horse people have a more realistic idea of the what is expected of them, the uninitiated students and hobbyists don't realize that almost every aspect of the horse industry requires a lot of long hours of difficult, dirty, back-breaking work with no weekends, or holidays, or even time off for good behavior.

Horses require a lot of work, even if they are not being ridden. Unless you have lots of fenced pasture available with plenty of grass year round, or don't care how healthy your horses are, or plan to spend a lot of money on vet bills, you have to be at the barn to feed two to three times a day, *everyday* at the same times just like clockwork. Stalls have to be cleaned *everyday,* and stripped of all bedding and re-bedded at least once a month. Horses must have clean water one to two times a day, *everyday.* They have to be turned out, brought back in, rinsed off and have their feet picked out *everyday.* And *everyday* they have to be checked for illness and injury. And *everyday* you have to check the stalls and fences for damage, and make repairs immediately. When horses are sick or injured, they need someone to doctor their wounds, or walk them all night long, or force them into trailers in usually the worst weather imaginable to haul them to a clinic or hospital. When a horse is beyond hope, someone (most likely you) must hold his head and stroke his neck as he leaves this world. And then there is the cost.

Horses, regardless of their purchase price, cost a whole lot of money to maintain. On the average, horse owners spend almost $5,000 per year* not including tack, training, riding lessons, showing, or medical care beyond vaccinations, teeth floating and deworming. And this amount assumes that the owners are providing almost all of the labor. This is as sizable amount money and time. *(See below for an explanation of how this amount was determined.)*

Yearly Cost of Supporting the Average Horse
Not including tack, training, lessons, showing or medical care

Feed ($10 per week)	$ 520
Hay ($12 per week based on 3 bales @ $4 each)	624
Shavings ($16 per week based on 4 bags @ $4 each)	832
Grooming Supplies (fly spray, hoof treatments and shampoo)	142
Dewormer (12 per year @ $15 each)	180
Shoes (every 6 weeks @ $70 each)	2130
Vaccinations (2 per year @ $45 each)	90
Teeth Floating (2 per year @ $100 each)	200
Coggins (1 per year)	30
Total	$4,784

*Prices may vary according to region of the country, brands chosen, and other such factors.

Ultimately, however, the money, time and physical effort caring for horses require are not the greatest challenge in the horse industry. The single greatest challenge horse professionals face is dealing with people, particularly horse owners, and parents. It is a challenge because, generally speaking, most people who are drawn to work in the horse industry are better at developing relationships and communicating with horses than they are with people. Yet, I can think of no other industry that challenges people skills – communication, problem solving, and conflict resolution - more than the horse industry does. Most customers know little or nothing about horses or the horse industry. This ignorance creates enormous obstacles for equine professionals. In many cases, huge egos accompany the huge incomes required to support a horse habit; a combination that usually results in customers who don't think they need to learn anything because they think they already know it all. Many people assume that if they know enough to make a lot of money, they also know enough to tell a mere horse professional, who makes comparatively little, how to do his or her job. They equate bank balances with IQ's. So patience, tolerance and thick skin are traits one absolutely must have to succeed in a horse business.

Even if you have those skills, the reality is that working with horses and their owners/riders can drain you physically and emotionally, and, if you don't learn the business aspects of the industry, it can drain you economically as well. So, if you are considering a career in the horse industry, whether you have horse experience or not, you need to make an honest assessment of your skills, and of how much you are willing to give to your profession.

❖ Are you willing to work long hours lifting heavy bales of hay, water buckets and sacks of feed?

❖ Do you have the self-discipline to put your work before anything else 24 hours a day, 7 days a week?

❖ Are you willing to return to the barn at 2:00 am to tend to a colicing horse, walk him for 3 hours non-stop then spend another 2 hours in the pouring, freezing rain trying to get the horse on the trailer so you can transport him to the vet clinic?

❖ Are you willing to get dirty mucking out stalls in the freezing cold of winter and the scorching heat of summer?

❖ Are you willing to accept the emotional risk of having a horse in your care be injured or die?

❖ Are you willing to give up your weekends and holidays? How about leaving your boyfriend/girlfriend/husband/ wife/family to travel to shows that can last up to two months or more?

❖ Are you willing and able to deal with people who constantly challenge your expertise even though the only thing they know about horses is how to write a check to cover their bills?

❖ Are you willing and able to cope with parents who misguidedly place ribbons and advancing to new levels above safety? How about those who put so much pressure on the child that riding is no longer fun?

❖ Are you willing to learn as much as you can about riding instruction, training, horse care, barn maintenance, farrier science, and other aspects of your particular part of the horse industry?

❖ Are you willing to fish dead mice and rats out of water buckets and feed bins?

❖ Are you willing to treat your business as a real business instead of a hobby by learning everything you can about bookkeeping, record keeping, liability, insurance, pricing, marketing, advertising, public relations and all the other aspects of business management?

If you answer "no" to any of these questions, you may want to consider working for someone else who is, or find another field that is far less demanding than the horse industry. If you can answer yes to all of these questions, then chances are you have what it takes to make it in the horse industry as a self-employed professional.

Some of you, who don't have a lot of hands-on experience with horses, probably think that these questions are fictitious exaggerations of the demands caring for horses involves. Let me assure you that every last one of the situations in these questions is based on things I have personally seen preformed regularly by trainers, instructors, barn workers, barn managers, veterinarians and others; and I left out some of the more unpleasant tasks. Some of you may now be thinking, "It doesn't matter how gross or difficult it is, I won't need to do this because I'm going to just manage a barn or work in another area of the business." Let me warn you, regardless of what area of the horse industry you work in, with the exception of advertising sales for equine publications, equine organizations, pharmaceutical, insurance, tack or feed sales, chances are very good that you will have to deal with many of these issues. If you are thinking you can avoid these tasks by hiring others, guess again. When you are running a horse business, the ultimate responsibility falls on your shoulders, so when the people you have hired to do the dirty work don't show up, as frequently happens, then you are the one who must take over. Even if you plan on working in ad sales, appraising, tack shops, feed or pharmaceutical sales, chances are very good that you will also put in long hours and need to know a good deal about bookkeeping, record keeping, liability, marketing etc.

If you are still reading this book, chances are that you are either in serious denial, or are so infected with the horse bug that you haven't been discouraged in your quest for a career involving horses. This being the case, it is time to decide just how you are going to create your business so that it will be a success for years to come.

Chapter Three

Determining Your Target Market

A business focus is vital to your success. The more clearly defined your business focus is, and the better you are at conveying that focus to existing and potential customers, the more successful you will be.

To begin developing a business focus, start by determining exactly what you are going to do to earn a living in the horse industry. While the first thoughts that pop into your mind might be of lesson programs, boarding operations, breeding farms, training or show facility, or tack shop, these are just the very broadest possibilities market segments. The first step in being successful is to narrow down your market to one of much smaller scope that will more clearly define your business focus.

Narrowing scope or market size is a concept that stops most people in business dead in their tracks. There is a real fear that narrowing their scope will cause them to leave money on the table by excluding potential clients. Their approach is to try to appeal to as many people as possible. Unfortunately, attempting to be all things to all people is the surest path to failure in any enterprise, even those that don't involve horses. When you attempt to go after the entire market place instead of a portion or segment of the total market, or if you try to go after too many similar markets, you fail to focus your energy, resources and message on attracting those consumers most likely to buy what you are selling.

While I do not have the statistics to back me up, I firmly believe that more businesses fail due to a lack of focus, than due to a lack of funding. No matter how much money you have or can borrow to start a horse business, without focus you are in big trouble.

To illustrate this point, let me tell you about two women who have been trying to get an equine assisted psychotherapy business off the ground for over two and a half years without much success. Both women are incredibly qualified with the appropriate degrees, training and licensing. They are very intelligent, likable, kind, caring, gentle people; just the perfect people to be doing what they are doing. They also had a good bit of money to get them started. Yet, after two and a half years of struggling, they called me because they were not making any headway. They were so frustrated and tired - mentally and physically- that they were ready to throw in the towel. They were also on the verge of financial collapse. I asked them to send me copies of all their marketing materials – flyers, brochures, news articles, advertisements, everything. A short review of these items made it very apparent that they had no clear focus. I couldn't tell if they were going after children suffering from attention deficit disorders, sexual or physical abuse, eating disorders, depression, self-confidence or relationship issues, or if they were going after adults with the same varied list of problems.

Without focus, it is impossible to really know what the service is that you are offering and neither will your customers.

If I couldn't tell, you can bet that their potential customers (their market) couldn't tell either. What's more they couldn't begin to present themselves to their potential customers in a way that would stimulate the customers to come to them for equine assisted psychotherapy instead of some one else. Without focus, they didn't really know what service they were offering and neither did their customers. Equine assisted psychotherapy is too broad a scope to keep the marketing focus interesting and personally meaningful to the potential customer. Without focus the business owners didn't really know who their best potential customers really were (the group with the greatest need, the income to pay to fill that need, and most likely to use their service), how the service was really beneficial to the customer, who their competition was, how to price their services so that they are more attractive to customers, where to locate themselves, where to place their advertisements, how to word their ads and other marketing materials.

They just kept stabbing in the dark going after all the people in their city who could possibly have a need for therapy with no clear idea of who had the greatest need and were the most likely to be interested in what they had to offer. Sometimes they hit the mark just enough to keep going but most of the time, they felt they were just spinning their wheels. Without a clearly defined focus, they could not begin to succeed. Fortunately, with a clear focus, they have a very good chance of building a successful equine assisted psychotherapy business as long as that focus is chosen based on solid facts instead of assumptions, personal prejudices or wishful thinking.

The Market

To better understand a business focus let's define what a **market, market segment** and **sub-segment** actually are. To put it in horse industry terms the **horse market** is everyone in the world who owns or is interested in owning or learning to ride a horse or doing something involving horses. A **segment of that market** would be everyone in the United States who owns or is interested in owning or learning to ride a horse or doing something involving horses. A **sub-segment** of the US horse market would be everyone who is interested in learning to ride, which can be broken down to everyone who is interested in learning to ride hunters. The hunter rider market can be further broken down to those hunter riders interested in pursuing national titles in hunter competition. This sub-segment can be broken down even further by location – all those in a particular state or town who are interested in winning national titles in hunter competition and so on down to all those females from 10 to 16 years of age residing in your town who are interested in winning national titles in hunter competition. This latter group is a well-defined and well-focused market; everyone in it has a similar interest, a similar age and will generally respond to similar marketing messages and benefits.

Focused Market Sub-Segment

Finding the properly focused sub-segment of a market really isn't as difficult as it may sound. To this point, your own interests have helped to narrow down your choice of the segment of the horse market that you want to provide products or services for.

For example: If you ride reining, and want to have a lesson program then you understandably want it to be a reining lesson program. You have the interest, experience and skills that you can pass on to your students. You also have some understanding of what a reining student is looking for in an instructor/trainer. You are wise to aim your business at the reining market in your area and even wiser if you narrow the focus even more to a particular age group, income or experience level. For instance, you could focus on only those reining riders who are interested in riding as a hobby, or only those who want to go after national titles. Or you may choose to go after beginning riders because you really prefer teaching young children who are just staring to ride. Regardless of the group you want to focus your business on, the narrower your scope, the more accurate your marketing and business efforts will be.

If you are a farrier, chances are that you are setting your sights on all the horse owners in your area, but you would be wiser to aim your sights at a smaller, more focused group such as performance horses. "Wait a minute," you might say in a panic, "if I limit myself to this group, look at all the horses I'm passing up." Yep, you'll be passing up the backyard horses, and the horses that are only ridden occasionally, and all those field trims that are the boil on most farriers' backsides. What you will be getting instead are clients who use their horses in competition, have generally

In a well focused market everyone in it has similar interests, age, income and will generally respond to the same marketing message and benefits.

Target market audience

– the portion of the market that you absolutely want to hit with an incredibly effective service, product or marketing campaign.

paid a lot to purchase these animals, and will generally pay more to have them shod by someone who really knows what he is doing. And if you are a really clever farrier, with a large enough horse population in your area; you will narrow your focus even further – specializing in hunter/jumpers and eventing horses. Now don't faint because you just lost the racehorses, barrel racers, etc. If there are more racehorses in your area than hunter/jumpers then narrow your focus to race horses, if there aren't enough horses used in a given discipline, then by all means go after all the performance horses. It really doesn't matter which group you focus on, all that matters is that you focus on a specific market that will benefit the most from your expertise, that you particularly want to work with and **that has enough people to support you**. And that you make this decision based on facts, not assumptions about the segment you are planning to focus on.

Keep in mind that the more selective your market is, the more skills they may require of you. So if you are going after a market segment that is willing to pay extra for expertise, then you will need to have that expertise.

When it comes to choosing your market segment, think in terms of a shotgun approach versus a rifle. With a shotgun, you don't have to be that accurate a shot. Shotguns can punch a lot more holes in a target than a rifle can even if all you do is point and shoot. The problem is that a shotgun punches a lot of little holes randomly placed, none of which are deadly in and of themselves, and the number of pellets that actually hit the bull's eye is very few. When using the shotgun approach for marketing you aim at everyone who has an interest in horses. You may hit a large number of them, but hitting those who are actually interested in the kind of lessons, or boarding program, or tack, or therapy you are selling (your bull's eye) with great enough consistency to make a good living is not all that likely. With a rifle you are only able to make one large hole in a target, but when properly fired at your bull's eye of a market the shot is absolutely on the mark every time, hitting the maximum number of people in your well-focused market segment. The rifle approach of marketing sets its sights on a very specific, well-defined market comprised of only those people who are most likely to want what you are selling. Hence the term **target market audience** – the portion of the market that you absolutely want to hit with an incredibly effective service, product or marketing campaign. The better defined the target market you are aiming for, the better you can design your business and marketing to "hit" that target with precision and convert your potential market into paying customers.

While the entire horse market is comprised of the largest number of people, trying to sell them on taking riding lessons at a hunter barn is a waste of time, effort and money. People who live in France aren't likely to fly to St. Louis, Missouri each week for a riding lesson. By the same token, horse owners in St. Louis who ride Western, love Western and want to compete in reigning aren't going to care that you are the best hunter instructor of all time. However, there are a lot of riders, particularly young girls from 5 to 16 years of age who have dreams of winning ribbons in the hunter ring and live in St. Louis, who would flock to the barn of the area's best hunter trainer. While the number of girls in this group may be small compared to the overall market, you are more likely to get them to come to you for lessons because of your skills, area of expertise and proximity, making them the target market segment that you need to focus on.

Whenever you begin a new business or have a business that is not doing well, the best course of action is to narrow your target market audience. When your business begins to grow and is on strong footing, then you can branch out to other sub-segments of your market. However, once you begin branching out, you have to do so with caution so that you don't confuse your original market and end up merely trading one market sub-segment for another. But that is not something you will need to worry about for some time.

If you narrow your focus properly and develop your business to fill an important need for your primary target market, you will be on solid footing to get your message out and bring customers to your door. In other words, if you focus on those potential customers that solid facts have proven exist, and that are the people you want to teach, or board, or train, or sell to, the more likely you are to design a service or product that will meet their need better than the competition does. Chances are that the members of this market segment will all value what you have to offer. They will all look to the same media for information, and be responsive to the same message making it easier, and more effective to reach them through advertising and other marketing methods.

The difficult part in narrowing your focus down is to choose the right size target market that is small enough to reach with one message, and still be large enough to build a profitable business. To do this you have to do your homework. Ideally this should be done as the first step to starting your business, before you buy the property, build a facility, lease office or retail space, order your first shipment of horseshoes, or hay. However, no matter how long you've been in business, if you don't have a narrow focus based on a study of your market, you need to develop one.

Whether you have an existing business or are starting a new one, the steps to narrowing your focus are exactly the same. You begin your homework by finding sources that provide you with vital information about the horse market in your area. (See: *Marketing Resources for Horse Businesses* at the back of this book.)

Where to Find Information

Breed and discipline organizations such as the American Quarter Horse Association, the American Reining Association, and the US Equestrian Federation are just a few of those that can tell you how many members they have in the area you want to service be it nationwide, state, county or city. These organizations can also tell you the complete **demographics** of their members.

Demographics

Demographics include age, income levels, educational background, riding habits and more information that is vital in helping you determine what a specific group's interest level may be in what you want to offer.

Demographics are a profile of a group. Demographics include age, income levels, educational background, riding habits and more information that is vital in helping you determine what a specific group's interest level may be in what you want to offer. In addition to breed and discipline organizations, a good source of demographic information is publications that cater to horse people such as Practical Horseman, Dressage Today, Horse & Rider, Arabian World, etc. You can acquire demographic information from organizations by going to their web site or calling to request a copy. It helps if you're a member of the organization or are willing to pay for their information. To receive a copy of demographics from a magazine that caters to the area of the market you are interested in, contact their advertising offices. Their contact information can be found in the area of the magazine know as the masthead – a narrow column headed by the name of the publication and a list of its publisher, editors etc, that is usually found in the first few pages of the magazine. When you contact advertising representatives, tell them that you are considering advertising in their publication and ask for a **media kit** with complete reader demographics. This information is typically given free of charge and can often be found on the publication's web site.

Keep in mind that the demographics from organizations and magazines are a rough number that tells only part of the story about your particular market. Their demographics include only those people who subscribe to their particular magazine or are members of their particular organization, not everyone in your area in a given discipline; not everyone who rides belongs to an organization or reads a magazine. Also, generally speaking these demographics are based only on those who answered the survey and not the entire membership or subscribers. Despite these facts, demographics collected by publications and organizations do give a pretty good idea of how many folks in your area are interested in what you have to offer and gives you a rough idea of what these folks are like.

The real numbers of potential and existing customers are often 10% - 60% higher than association memberships and magazine

10% - 60% higher than association memberships and magazine subscriptions indicate. However, in some instances such as riding lesson programs, the people who are willing to pay for lessons are generally the same people who pay for association memberships and read magazines targeted to a particular discipline. They tend to be more passionate about their riding, want to improve and are willing to pay to do so. Keep in mind that this is true of *existing* riders. Children and adults, who are dreaming of riding, don't usually belong to organizations. They typically join after they start lessons. Still the demographics of riding organization members and horse magazine subscribers will give you an idea of how many young riders there are presently competing in your area, what kind of horses they own and other valuable pieces of information.

Other good sources of useful demographic information are the American Horse Council, your own state horse council, the US Department of Agriculture, your state Department of Agriculture, county agent, and colleges of agriculture. These organizations often offer profiles of the horse industry nationally, state and county wide, and locally. These profiles are generally known as "Horse Industry Economic Impact Studies." Impact studies are filled with all kinds of information including where the largest concentration of horses is in your region, the number of training and lesson programs, tack shops, farriers and more. You can usually request copies of the latest horse industry impact studies by visiting the web sites of these organizations. Some allow you to download the information for free, while others charge for it. If there is a fee, don't let that stop you as this can be invaluable information for formulating business plans, structuring your business, and crafting your marketing strategies making it one of the most vital tools you need to get your business off to a good start, or to help turn it into a profitable business.

The information from horse related sources and the general census is useful in determining if the geographical area you want to work in has enough potential customers to support you.

However, before you spend a lot of money, ask for a listing of the kind of information contained in the study. If it doesn't provide specifics relevant to your target market audience or geographical area, it may not be of any use to you. For instance if the study doesn't include the number of barns and a break down of lesson programs by discipline, it may not be much help if you want to open a lesson program. But if the study includes the average age of riders of a certain discipline in your state and where they are located, this can be very useful.

Once you have the demographic information together, you can sit down and see if the number of potential customers in a specific market segment or sub-segment is sufficient to support your business.

You next need to discover the overall population for the area you want to work in and, if possible, determine how many males, and females grouped by age and income reside in that area. You can generally get this information from a local chamber of commerce or through the state census.

What you are hoping to find in all of the information from horse related sources and the general census is if the geographical area you want to work in has a reasonably large number of existing riders and potential riders, or in the case of EAP businesses enough people with a given emotional, behavioral or communication problem.

Once you have an idea of how many existing and potential customers are in a given area, it is time to take a look at all of your competition. How many similar businesses are servicing or trying to service the same people you want to focus on? What can you offer that they can't? Can you do a better job in less time, for less money? Will you be the first one to cater to a particular market segment? All of these considerations are important to determining your business focus, or if you should open a horse business in the area you were considering or look elsewhere, or find another business focus.

Demographics and Your Primary Business Focus

An example of the value of using demographic information to determine your primary business focus is a client who has a girl's school with a riding program. Although the existing program was hunter/jumper based, a parent who rides eventing insisted that hunter/jumper was a waste of time and that the school should be focused on eventing. Contacting the US Eventing Association and the US Equestrian Federation showed that there were more than three times as many hunter/jumper riders in the school's state than there were eventing riders, particularly among riders 18 years and under – the age group most likely to attend the school. This clearly demonstrated that the school should not change their focus if they wanted to continue to build their riding program because there were more hunter/jumper riders in the area in which they recruited the majority of their students.

Another example of how to use demographics to effectively determine what sort of business you want to set up and where you want to locate would be a fictitious hunter barn.

Let's say that you are a very good hunter seat equitation rider with a long history of competitive riding. You decide you want a career teaching other hunter seat riders. You go to college and get a degree in Equine Studies and instructor certification through the American Riding Instructor Association for good measure. You decide you want to work with those students who are intermediate to advanced riders who want to pursue the Medal Maclay. You pick three geographical areas that you would want to live and work in. You then contact the US Equestrian Federation and find out how many hunter riders under the age of 17 are members of their organization who reside in these three areas. You discover that the largest number is in Hunterville. You then investigate Hunterville, which has a population of 800,000 and discover that 18% of the population or 144,000 are females 18 and under. You also find that the US Equestrian Federation has 5,000 members in this age group who reside in Hunterville. Your research also uncovers that there are 200 hunter seat instructors or one for every 25 students and at least half of those instructors have qualifications similar to yours. Even though it is a large market, the facts indicate that the competition is very stiff, and that there may not be enough students to support one more instructor.

According to the US Equestrian Federation's demographics, the second largest group of hunter riders – 2,500 is St. Jumper – overall population 500,000 and of that 16% or 80,000 are females 18 and under. On further investigation, you discover that in St. Jumper there are 50 hunter instructors or one instructor for every 50 riders and only four other instructors in the area have qualifications similar to yours.

The third town you picked, Ponyopolis has an overall population of 200,000 of that 22% or 44,000 are females 18 and under. Ponyopolis has the fewest number of USEF hunter seat riders with only 200. In Ponyopolis there are only two hunter instructors (one instructor for every 100 riders), neither of whom have anything close to your qualifications. In this example, even though it has the smallest overall population and the smallest number of riders who belong to USEF, Ponyopolis may have the greatest opportunity for someone with lots of qualifications to run a riding program aimed at young riders hoping to reach the Medal Maclay finals. The only thing that could drastically change this picture is the number of people in Ponyopolis who earn over $50k per year.

Making it to the Medal Maclay takes a sizeable investment and if there aren't enough people in a given area who make that kind of money, it is fairly certain that you won't have enough clients to make a living catering to this market segment. However, if you alter your focus to aiming at kids who may want to rider hunter equitation at schooling and maybe a few rated shows each year, you may be able to do extremely well in Ponyopolis. Of course, if Ponyopolis is populated mainly by folks whose only interest is Western Pleasure, you may have to give up and go elsewhere. In the end, realistically you can only make such decisions if you have statistical facts that show you what the market is really like before you spend the money to move there and set up your business.

Equine Assisted Psychotherapy

If you are planning to open an equine assisted psychotherapy business, you need to focus more on finding out information about the mental health care market than you do about the horse market. To do so, contact the local chapters of state or national organizations that address the particular mental health care issues you want to treat. Ask them how many members they have in your area broken down by age groups, gender, education and income.

To discover who is presently treating these mental health care issues, contact your state licensing agencies and ask for a list of their members in the state. If you are only interested in servicing an individual town or metropolitan area, you will need to know how many individual counselors, therapists, psychologists, psychiatrists and treatment facilities there are in the area. You should be able to get this information from the various licensing agencies and the phone book.

As you may need to market to the mental health care providers to get them to send you referrals or to use your services as an adjunct to theirs, you will need to break down the providers by type of services they offer and areas of specialization such as behavior disorders, eating disorders, family counseling, marriage counseling, etc. If you find that very few treat a specialty you were hoping to offer, such as attention deficit disorder, it wouldn't make much sense for you to look to the local mental health care providers to send you customers. However, if no one in the area is servicing children with this disorder, you might be wise to tailor your service to fill the gap. You won't know any of this unless you do your research.

What Your Existing Customers Can Tell You

Remember the two ladies with the struggling, unfocused equine assisted psychotherapy business? To help them narrow their focus, I suggested that they review all their past customers to see what particular disorder, age, income and other aspects they had in common. The ladies then picked the top two – sexual abuse and attention deficit disorder. This allowed them to contact various organizations to discover the number of cases of each condition that occurs each year in their town. Once those numbers were uncovered, they then made a list of all the treatment options and providers there were in their town that addressed them. They finally decided on tailoring their EAP business to address the one that had the largest number of cases and the fewest treatment options.

Keep in mind that there are occasions throughout your business's life when you may have to narrow your focus further or change your focus altogether as the market changes. For example: you have a thoroughbred-breeding program for dressage riders. Your target market audience begins buying warm bloods. You have to either begin breeding warm bloods or change your target market audience to one that is still using thoroughbreds. Or if you are a farrier specializing in reigning and dressage horses and the number of such horses declines while the number of jumpers or race horses in your area increases, then you better shift your focus or sell your forge. Regardless of what target market audience you start with, you can and must change it when needed to respond to shifts in riding styles, tastes and trends.

To start and continue to run a successful business, you must choose your market segment so that is has the proper focus but keep your eyes out for changes in your market and be ready to act accordingly. A commitment has to exist between you and your market, but it doesn't have to be a lifetime commitment. While you're committed to one market, you need to keep a close watch to make sure that if the market changes you change with it to meet its new needs or get yourself a new market.

Direct Competitors are all those business going after the same people you are going after.

To get an idea of your potential market and the segment you want to focus on go to the form *The Size and Composition of Your Potential Market* on pages i - iv in the Appendix.

The Competition

What are the other guys in your business doing to service the market segment you want? What goods or services are they offering? Are they emphasizing quality, price, service or something else? Are they servicing the whole market or is there a portion of the market that they may be under-servicing? How can you do it better? Will you be the first in your area to offer a particular service or product? Do you have a new spin on an old idea? Have you come up with something completely original, a never-before-seen idea? All of these are important in helping you determine who your competition actually is and how best to stand out from them.

It is surprising that most businesses have an extremely limited view of who the competition actually is. Generally business people tend to think that their only "competitors" are those businesses that offer the same goods or services they do. The truth is that your competitors are all those businesses that aim at your market or market segment. Competitors fall into two categories, direct competitors and indirect competitors.

Direct Competitors are all those horse related business going after the same pocket books that belong to the same people you are going after. **Indirect competitors** are all those non-horse goods and services that appeal to your market who might get their money instead of your.

Ultimately a competitor is anyone who is trying to divert money that could be yours even if the competitor is in another market altogether. So when considering your competition, it is wise to consider both direct and indirect competitors.

In the case of tack shops, farriers, equine vets, and other suppliers of horse products and services, these indirect competitors may not be much of a problem because, while they may divert some customers, they don't really have much impact on pricing. However, riding instructors are not so fortunate. Of all the professions in the horse industry, the one group most affected by indirect competitors is riding instructors.

How good a job or product your competitor offers is of far less importance than how good a job they do marketing themselves and their product.

While horse shoers may have to contend with clients who choose one month to buy themselves a pair of shoes instead of their horse, or a breeder might lose a sale to buyers deciding to take a cruise instead of buying a new horse, riding instructors can temporarily or permanently lose a student to any sport team or after school activity in their town. The price these indirect competitors charge for lessons and training in a town can also set a limit on how much a riding instructor can reasonably charge for lessons. So when it comes to riding instructors, it is crucial to know what teams and individual sports, and art, dance, and music programs are available in your area that are aiming at your market segment. Riding instructors also need to know how much each of these activities costs and what advantages they offer the market segment the riding instructor is focusing on. Once the riding instructor has this information, it can be used to determine pricing, packaging and promoting a lesson program.

Sizing Up Your Competition

When it comes to sizing up your competition, do not fall into the trap of dismissing those direct and in-direct competitors that you feel are offering sub-standard goods or services. How good a job or product your competitor offers is of far less importance than how good a job they do marketing themselves and their product. There are a few arrogant trainers I know who think that they don't have any competition because they are just so much better than everyone else. Even if they are the very best trainer in the world, all the other trainers that are marketing to the same customer are competitors. All it takes to steal business from the leader in any field is for the competition to find the leader's weakness and go after it with a brilliant marketing campaign. No matter how good a company or individual is, they can be vulnerable to the competition no matter how small or apparently inferior the competition may be. (Take a look at McDonalds who, after decades of leading the fast food industry, are now reporting losses. Their mistake was to ignore changes in the fast food market while their competitors didn't. Despite constant headlines about fast food's contribution to the growing problem of obesity in America, McDonalds did little more than add salads to their menu. Meanwhile, Subways has been promoting all the people who have lost huge amounts of weight eating nothing but their sandwiches.)

The other side of that coin is to dismiss those who think they are the best even when all they are really better at is getting the market to believe what they are telling them, in other words they are better at marketing and self-promotion than they are at training horses and riders. To dismiss these folks is foolish if you want to build a successful horse business. Typically, the response I have seen most horse professionals take in dealing with these self-promoters is to point out all their flaws to their own customers or sometimes anyone else who will listen. This tactic is not only unprofessional; it sends your customers the message that this self-promoter threatens you. Often your customers will begin to think that if you are so threatened then maybe the self-promoter is actually better. So be aware that the quality or lack of quality of your competitors doesn't make them competitors, it is the fact that they are after the same customers you are that makes them competitors. The best way to win in this battle is to never say anything bad about them, instead devote your time and energy into developing a business that better understands the customer, and that does a better job at meeting their needs. But before you can beat the enemy, you have to know who the enemy actually is.

The ideal way to size up your competition is find out everything you can about them. Don't just rely on rumors or second hand reports. Take the time to visit the competition's place of business. Review back issues of publications they advertise in to get a feel for what they think their strongest benefits are. Find out everything you can about the services they offer and what they charge for them. There is nothing wrong with calling up the competition, pretending to be a customer looking for a product or service and asking lots of questions. Visit their web sites and look at how easy the sites are to use, and the kind of information they contain. Go to horse shows and observe the competition in action. If you are a riding instructor, check with local parenting and horse publications, the phone book, the classified section of the local newspaper, your city's web site, the library, etc. to see who your in-direct competitors are, what they are offering and how they are marketing themselves.

Get a map of your area and circle those neighborhoods that are populated by your target market audience - chosen because of your research indicates that your potential customers live there.

Put a red "X" to mark the location of all of your direct competitors and a different color "X" to mark the location of all of your in-direct competitors even if they work out of their home. The idea is to give yourself an idea of how many competitors your clients and potential clients have to pass to get to you. Realize that even if a competitor is not in direct line between you and your customers, if they are closer geographically to the customer than you are, they are considered to be between you and your customers.

The key is to be different from the competition in a way that either addresses a need no one else does or to do the same thing better.

Make a list of what these competitors offer, and how much they charge. Make an honest assessment of their strong points and weaknesses. When making these evaluations you need to be very honest and not look at them through your own prejudices and jealousies. If someone has a really nice facility that is clean and well run, it is wise to recognize it, and, if necessary, bring your facility up to the same standards. If they are a good trainer, or instructor, even if you don't like them personally, you need to admit their strengths. If a facility appears to be beautiful and more posh than anything you can ever hope to afford, don't let it blind you to weaknesses such as a very high incident of colic, or high boarder turnover. If a tack shop is part of a big national chain then their strength may be price and variety, but their weakness may be poor service. Regardless, it is imperative that you deal with facts to create as realistic picture of your competition as you have of your customer. Once you really understand your competition, you will know how to better shape your business and your marketing to take customers from the competition while preventing them from taking yours.

> To get an idea of who your competitors are, use the form **Sizing Up the Competition** on pages vii of the Appendix.

Vision: How You Want Others to See You

Having a clear vision of how you want customers, potential customers and even the competition to see you is an important part of shaping your business and how your market it. The key is to be different from the competition in a way that either addresses a need no one else does or to do the same thing better. Do you want to be considered *Safer, more professional?* Do you want to emulate a leader in another field, to be *the Wal-Mart of tack or the Harvard of equine colleges?* Do you see yourself as more public service oriented by *helping the beginning rider to the next level* or *helping horse owners keep their animals sound?* What is your business about – *It's about riding not ribbons* or *It's about being the best rider you can be*? Do you want to be seen as the winner in some contest – *The leaders in show management*? What is the very essence of your business – *XYZ Farms means good-natured, healthy horses*? What do you want to be famous for- *the largest number of national champions in your hometown or state or the country* or *the happiest riders* or *the best customer service?* Knowing what you want people to think, dreaming big about who you want to be, is the surest way to making that dream come true and to standing out from the competition.

Whatever you want to be, the minutes you spend thinking about the impression you want people to have of you is time well spent because how you want to be seen greatly affects the way you shape your business. The better defined your vision is, the better your business will project the image you want. Once you have a clear vision, every decision about your business should consider how it will affect the image you are trying to project.

For example: If your vision is to be the leading show barn in your area, you should buy professionally made tack stall curtains before you attend your first horse show. Your purchase should be the type of curtains that a leading show barn would buy, not the tack curtains of someone just starting out with a small budget. Like an actress auditioning for a role, the best way to get the part is to look the part. No one is going to hire a sloppy, poorly dressed woman to play the role of a queen anymore than someone looking for a top trainer will chose a trainer who has homemade or shabby tack curtains.

If your vision is to be the barn with the happiest riders, then every decision should be based on how it will contribute to that goal. What kinds of trails will your riders enjoy more? What kinds of activities can you offer that your riders will enjoy? What kind of pictures will you use in your promotional materials – riders with serious faces or big smiles? (Smiles of course, we're a happy barn.) What kind of font will you use in your logo? All of these things should be determined by your vision and should reinforce that vision.

> **Tip:** Vision statements can make great slogans. Use them along with your logo at the bottom of printed ads or at the end of radio or television ads to reinforce your benefit to the customer.

Positioning, takes your vision and your focus a step further to ensure that your existing and potential customers perceive you to be the leader in your area of expertise.

> For help in determining your vision see **Vision: How You See Yourself Determines How the Customer Sees You** on page vii of the Appendix.

Positioning Yourself for Maximum Impact

As we have already discussed, knowing yourself and how the market sees you is critical to building a thriving business. With positioning, you can take your vision and your focus a step further to ensure that your existing and potential customers perceive you to be the leader in your area of expertise.

> **For example:** If you own a trail riding business - it is very difficult to sell yourself as a general trail riding service. You won't stand out in your customers' mind and in all likelihood you will be passed over. However, if

the customer perceives you as "The Trail Ride for Families," you will have a great deal of appeal to families looking for a trail ride for their weekends or vacations. Even if your competition also caters to mostly families, if they aren't using that fact in their advertising and you are, guess who the families are going to turn to?

If you have a carriage service and you sell yourself as "The carriage ride for honeymooners or those who would like to be," you are suddenly standing out away from the pack. The key to positioning is the same as discovering your focus, you have to understand what services you are offering, those you can offer and who is most likely to buy these services.

General Rule of Positioning: If you are not the first one in the category; i.e. carriage rides, then you should be the first to sell yourself as a special sub-category; i.e. carriage rides for honeymooners. If you are not the first roping barn in the area, then you should be the first to sell yourself as a trainer for professionals, or working ranchers.

Goals

Imagine playing a game of basketball without a goal or running a race with no finish line. The only way to gauge how well you are doing, or how much progress you have made, or how well you are keeping up with the competition is by setting goals. Goals may include things such as the number of students, customers or horses you want to have, the number of horse shows or trail rides you would like to attend or conduct, how much you want to increase your revenues, additional training you would like to have, how much you want to expand your facility, implementing a new record keeping system, improving your arena etc.

Goals are very personal. The only thing that matters in choosing your goals is that they really mean something to you, that they are something you want to accomplish, and will be proud of once you do.

Once you determine your goals, consider how you will reach them. Formulate your plan by breaking large goals down into smaller more immediately attainable goals. For instance, if your goal is to build a larger arena, then your first goal might be to have new post holes dug within 5 days, followed by setting all the new fence posts by the end of the following week. The more you can break goals down, the easier it is to get things done and with each step completed you will have a better sense of control and accomplishment that will keep you going. Setting a time limit also helps significantly; just remember that time limits should be reasonable. If you don't give yourself adequate time to reach a goal, you may be setting yourself up for disappoint, frustration and a real sense of failure, none of which is conducive to reaching your goals. So set a time limit but make sure the limit is attainable.

Don't be afraid to ask for help in reaching your goals. Family members and friends are often more than willing to help even if all they can provide is moral support. If you have employees, partners or co-workers they need to be involved in choosing the goals because they will ultimately play a part in helping you reach them. They are more likely to do so if they had a hand in setting the goals. Don't forget your customers either, especially if you are shaping your goals around meeting their needs. Why build a new arena if the majority of customers feel that you need better trails instead?

Once your goals are set, keep them in a place where everyone who has a hand in reaching them will see them everyday – taped to the computer monitor or filing cabinet in your office, the refrigerator at home, a bulletin board, the visor in your car or truck, your bathroom mirror or any place that you are going to see more than once a day. The more often you see your goals, the more likely you are to reach them. Keep in mind that not all goals should be shared with customers, employees or visitors to your place of business. Use good judgment and don't place any goals on your list that might have a negative impact on your customers. If you do, keep the list where you are the only person likely to see it.

> **Tip:** Long-range goals are not set in concrete. They can and should be changed as competition, the market place and other circumstances require.

For help in setting your goals see *GOALS: Where Is Your Business Headed* on page x of the Appendix.

Liability and Risk

I am sure that you are probably asking yourself what liability and risk have to do with marketing. Aside from the liability and risk of making false claims in your advertising, and perhaps some risk from being sued for saying something bad about a competitor, liability and risk should be a big part of your marketing. Although most college courses in marketing will not tell you this or even agree with me about the importance of liability and risk in relation to your marketing, I can assure you that, if you don't pay close attention to liability and risk in every aspect of your business, you face the very real prospect of not having a business, a home or an income.

Sadly, we have become a nation of lawsuits. Far too many people look at lawsuits as if they are the lottery – a quick way to make a fortune. And the odds of winning a lawsuit are far greater than the odds of winning the lottery. So as you build the foundation to your business, it is imperative that you consider the liability and risk aspects before you open your doors to customers.

If you don't pay close attention to liability and risk in every aspect of your business, you face the very real prospect of not having a business, a home or an income.

You may think that because your state has an equine activities sponsor limited liability law that you are automatically protected. Let me assure you that this may not be the case. The most important thing for you to do is to have copies of all the laws in your state that relate to horses and their owners, from land use to horse waste disposal to equine activities limited liability laws, and that you comply with those laws. I strongly urge you to have an attorney, who is well versed in both defendant personal injury law and the equine laws of your state, draft releases and contracts for you. (A web site where you can obtain all such laws in your state is provided in the back of this book – Liability and Risk Issues.) I also recommend that you acquire copies of Equine *Law and Horse Sense* and *More Equine Law and Horse Sense*, both written by Julie Fershtman, an expert in equine liability law. It is a good idea to take these books along with copies of all of your state's horse laws to the attorney whom you hire to draft your releases and contracts.

If you don't pay your taxes, you risk huge fines and penalties and possibly land you in jail.

And, while you may not see the need or even like helmets, I urge you to personally wear an ASTM/SEI certified helmet especially went mounted and to make it a requirement that your students do so as well, particularly any one that is under the age of 21. Ask your attorney how to protect yourself, if any adult rider does not want to wear such a helmet or if the parent of a student under 21 refuses to have her child wear such a helmet. Not only can it save lives and prevent serious, life-altering injuries, it can save your business, farm, home and life savings.

Taxes, Permits & Licenses

Although this is a dirty word, and may seem to have no place in a book about marketing or making money with your horse business, paying your taxes regularly and on time can make or break your business. If you are a self-employed horse person, regardless of what kind of business you have, you are required by federal and state laws to regularly pay some form of self-employment tax or withholding taxes. If you don't pay them in a timely and appropriate fashion, the government will impose huge fines and penalties that may cost you your property, your horses and your tack, and possibly land you in jail. So be responsible and pay your taxes. If you have employees, you need to take care of their withholding taxes as well. To do it right may take more effort and cost you more than you intended but in the long run, not doing taxes correctly can cost you far more. For tax information, contact your accountant, state offices of revenue and taxation and the US Internal Revenue Services. You should be able to find the information you need on their web sites.

Almost every city or township requires all businesses to have permits. You may have to register with you state attorney general or your city clerk of court. There is usually a fee required that can range from a few dollars to several hundred depending on the laws and requirements of your particular area or business. Your state Department of Agriculture may also have some kind of permitting requirement; check with them to find out what they may be.

Licensing requirements also vary state to state depending on the service, or products, or type of business. In some states, trainers and riding instructors are required to have a license. You will have to check with your individual state to determine if your particular profession or business requires a license.

Don't try to side step licensing or you might have your business shut down for non-compliance and have to pay huge fines. Despite what you may think, ultimately it is easier, and cheaper to do things the correct way from the beginning.

Chapter Four

Pricing: Deciding What to Charge

The horse industry is comprised of businesses that sell tangibles – tack, horses, feed, and other products, and those that sell intangibles – riding lessons, board, transportation, advertising, college education, equine assisted psychotherapy and other services. In either situation the inability to set prices properly is ultimately one of the major reasons horse businesses fail. In the end it doesn't matter how good a job you do of selling your services or goods, if you aren't making enough money per transaction, you will not make enough to stay in business.

I have worked with haulers, farriers, riding programs, boarding stables, trainers and other horse related business owners who have no clue how to use costs to set price. Most of them just look at what the competition is charging and copy them. Sometimes this method works, but all too often it is a disaster. A person who purchased property or a riding facility more than 10 or more years before you won't have the same costs on their shoulders as you will if you are buying a similar facility at today's market value. Chances are that they will be able to charge less than you can because of this one item.

Not too long ago a riding program at a school was showing huge losses. They looked to marketing, to attracting new students as the answer. Before addressing this issue, a budget review was called for. If they weren't making money with their existing students and horses, new students may not solve the problem. After taking a quick look at the budget, it was evident that the per-semester fee for the riding program was part of the problem. When the overall fee was broken down to a per lesson charge it amounted to about $8 per lesson. The going rate for riding lessons in the area ranged from $15 to $50 per lesson. A self-taught backyard trainer was offering the lower priced lessons and the higher priced lessons were taught by someone with slightly more experience than the school's instructor but with far less equine specific education. According to the school's administration, no one had any idea how the original fee structure was ever determined. No one ever reevaluated the costs to determine if they needed to adjust the pricing. If we had gotten them a lot more students at

$8 per lesson, the school's riding program would have continued to lose money because it was costing them more than $8 per lesson to provide them.

For those of you who sell products there are already set formulas for setting price at percentages above your original costs. As these formulas have been created over years of experience, you would be wise to follow them. However, you should keep in mind that your vision of yourself may have some impact on your pricing. If you want to be the Wal-Mart of feed, for instance, then offering discounts and going for volume may be the way to go. Even then you have to consider all your other operating costs in addition to the cost of each item before you can best determine the price of each items. In any case, there are numerous organizations designed specifically to help retailers and you would be wise to take advantage of any pricing assistance they may offer.

You can't stay in business if your income isn't more than your expenses.

When it comes to those in the horse industry who are selling intangibles, things are not quite so easy. There may be set prices but quite often they are nothing more than the going rate, with no one having a clue as to what these rates were based on. There are no special formulas or organizations to provide pricing guidance. Horse professionals who work with intangibles are pretty much on their own to figure things out and the results can be disastrous.

The issue of setting price can be an involved and complicated process. The goal here is to make it as simple as possible. First it is important to understand that you can't stay in business if your income isn't more than your expenses. That may seem basic to some, but it is interesting how often the basics are overlooked.

To help you determine your costs and your income use *Pricing: **Part I - Determining your costs*** and *Pricing: **Part II - Determining Your Income*** on pages xv and xvi of the Appendix. These forms may be adapted to your individual business. For instance if you are a farrier your expenses would include all those costs attached to your equipment including gasoline for your truck to take you to various clients, forge maintenance and fuel, shoes, nails etc. You may not have any expenses for a facility and therefore won't need to fill in those cost items. The key here is to make a list of everything you have to have and pay for in order to conduct your business.

Charging What You Are Worth

Of all the phobias I encounter with horse business owners, particularly those who offer a service, the one phobia that is probably the most insidious and detrimental is the fear of charging what something is worth. Time and again I encounter riding instructors, and equine assisted psychotherapists, and countless other horse professionals, who are too timid to price themselves at a rate that will provide a living wage.

One of my clients has a degree in equine studies from a leading equine college, is accredited to teach through advanced levels in hunter/hunter equitation by the American Riding Instructor Association and has over 20 years of successful showing experience. Despite all of these qualifications, she was concerned that if she charged more than the mid-range for her area, even though she had more qualifications than the competition, that she would not get any students. The most difficult part of helping her market her business was convincing her that if she marketed her lesson program to the right market she could ask for and get the highest fees in her market area. She just had to focus on the right market and get over her timidity and false modesty. She had the qualifications to draw students who are serious about their riding and who want to ride in rated shows. How seriously do you think such students would take her, if she charged what backyard trainers were charging? Quite often customers consider the size of the fees charged with the ability of the person offering the service. This is true of instructors, trainers, clinicians, farriers, haulers, therapists, etc.

All too often, pricing is more of a reflection of the business owner's self-worth than it is a reflection of their cost of doing business or other such financial realities.

The other side of that coin is the instructor who has an overblown sense of self-worth and charges too much, expecting to get top fees without having the qualifications or results to justify them. So when it comes to setting fees for services, be very honest about your qualifications. If you want to make the big bucks you have to have the substance to justify it and the courage to charge what you are worth.

Ultimately, pricing needs to be about covering your costs and making enough to live on. All too often, pricing is more of a reflection of the business owner's self-worth than it is a reflection of their cost of doing business or other such financial realities. If you get caught in the trap of letting emotions control your pricing, you may not stay in business long. If you don't think what you are offering is of genuine value, quit now and find another job doing something, anything that you do feel has value.

Profit Margins

Your Profit Margin is simply the money you have left over after all expenses have been taken care of in relation to your overall income. If your business has an income of $100,000 in a year and expenses of $75,000, your profit margin is $25,000, or 25% of your total income is pure profit. 25% is an excellent profit margin in any business and all too often unheard of in horse related businesses. The primary reason for this is that too little attention is paid to setting prices based on expenses.

If you have pricing problems, take heart in knowing that you are not alone. Even Fortune 500 companies are constantly battling to keep income ahead of expenses. It is a process that requires diligence but the energy is well spent if it keeps your profit margins high enough to provide a decent living.

Profit margins are also important in determining what to charge and how to shape your business so that it is as profitable as possible. For instance, if you run a lesson program, your income from those lessons may only have a 10% profit margin, but horse shows may net you 25% -30% profit with fees for schooling, day-care, etc. When it comes to making more money for less effort, horse shows may be the way to go. Of course you have to have a lesson program to build the showing part of your business.

No matter what your present profit margin may be, realize that today's profit margin is a starting point for building for the future. Even if you are operating at a loss, don't be discouraged. By making a few critical changes, you can turn your business into one that will provide you with a reasonable income.

A good profit margin to aim for is 12% to 20%. To increase your profit margins to this level may require that you increase your charges for services, increase your services or cut costs. Cutting cost is usually the first place businesses look to increase profits. While this is may seem the best choice, it is the wrong step if it requires you to reduce the quality of services you provide. The thing to keep in mind is how cutting the costs will affect your Vision and your long-term goals. The best rule of thumb in a service oriented business is not to cut what you spend on those items that can significantly affect the quality of services you offer your customers. When you are selling service, the customer expects to receive the same quality of service that brought them to you in the first place.

Generally speaking, instead of just jumping in and cutting costs, the wiser choice is usually to increase prices or expand those services that are operating at the highest profit margin levels.

For example: If your lesson program is operating at a 25% profit margin while your board business is only netting you 10%, increase your lesson program or find an additional service to offer your boarders that will increase your overall board income.

To find out which aspect of your business has the highest profit margin, you will need to break your business down into the various parts for which you charge a fee, and determine the costs and incomes from each part.

For example: If you have an equine assisted psychotherapy business, you can break your business down to regular sessions, workshops, retreats and special presentations. If you run a lesson barn, you can break your business down by group lessons, private lessons, horse shows. Each one of these services is structured differently, has a different fee schedule and should be considered separately. This should help you discover how much income and profit each segment generates during a business year and make it easier for you to see where the bulk of your profit actually comes from.

No matter what business you are in, it is very important that you know which aspects of your business are making you money and which ones are losing you money. Only then can you realistically decide whether you are wiser to improve this particular aspect, increase the price you charge for it, or drop it all together and devote more time to those things that generate the highest profit margins.

TIP: Don't overlook packaging as another way to increase profits or cash flow from a particular part of your business. For example: if you are a farrier you may be able to make more money if you sell a package of 10 shoeings for a price that is an overall savings of 10% - (10 shoeings may generally sell for $600 but if you sell the package for 10% less or $540, you will have a whole lot more money to put in the bank than the $60 you usually get for a single shoeing. This means that you may be able to reduce your overhead by purchasing a piece of equipment you need with cash or paying off a loan that you wouldn't be able to if you were just getting the price of a single shoeing at each billing. In the long run the ability to pay cash for needed equipment or pay off a higher interest loan sooner, may save you more than the $60 discount you give your customer as an incentive for advanced payment. Plus you won't have the aggravation of writing up 10 individual bills and tracking down the payment of each one.

You can do the same thing with lesson plans, training packages, hauling fees, and even equine assisted psychotherapy sessions. Getting large sums of money in advance that reduces paperwork, collection time and allows you to pay on loans or pay cash for needed equipment, can be well worth any reasonable discount you offer your customers.

Additional training as a means of increasing profit is perhaps the most overlooked area in the horse business, or any business. Yet, training that leads to professional certification can mean that your customers may be more than willing to pay more for your services as compared to the same services offered by uncertified equine business professionals. Further, training that makes it possible for you to conduct your business with greater efficiency or safety can increase your profit margin. For example: An equine nutrition class that teaches you how to better feed your horses may lead to you using more hay and less feed. The end result is that your horses cost you less to feed and are healthier, which means a reduction in vet bills and overall expenses. Or if you go through the process of earning a professional certification, it could result in you having to pay less for professional insurance. Best of all additional professional training is generally tax-deductible.

> To help you assess your present profit margin, use Pricing: *Determining Your Present Profit Margin* on page xvii of the Appendix.

The Business Plan

A good business plan is not just a nice thing to do to help you run your business, it is absolutely necessary if you want to succeed.

These days a good business plan is not just a nice thing to do to help you run your business, it is absolutely necessary if you want to succeed. You cannot get a loan; apply for grants, special tax exemptions and such unless you have a business plan. I personally, can't imagine how anyone who hopes to succeed in business would overlook writing a business plan as the single most important component of building a strong foundation for your business. Formulating a good business plan forces you to consider all aspects of your business and to use facts rather than opinion or assumption to shape your business.

As important as it is, most people starting out in business and even a number of long-time business owners are overwhelmed by the idea of putting together business plans. Just like pricing there are volumes of books on the market devoted to writing business plans. While I highly recommend you find one that works for you, many computer programs have templates for writing business plans that make the task easier. If you have MicroSoft Word 2003, you can download a really good business plan that helps you through the process. You will find it on the www.microsoft.com web site under templates. You can also find business plan writing software and other resources with a web search "business plans." There are even people who will write a business plan for you for a fee. Whatever it takes to get your business plan done, do it.

I cannot begin to tell you how important the business plan is to your success and to helping you make more money with less effort. You might be wondering why, given my feelings about the importance of developing a business plan, I've waited until now to bring it up. The answer is simple, if you have filled out all of the forms I've provided up to this point; you already have most of the information necessary to write a business plan. You can take the data you have collected on costs, income, profit margins, vision, goals, competition, and customer profiles and fill in the blanks on a business plan. If

I had started this book discussing business plans you might have tossed it aside. This way by telling you the benefits of each piece of the plan, you kept going. In other words, I tailored my product to fit my market. See how important it is to know your market?

Chapter Five

Marketing

Good marketing requires a multifaceted approach, which is just a fancy way of saying that marketing requires that you consider how everything you do in the course of running your business from the prospective of how it effects your marketing efforts. Marketing and promoting your business should become instinctive. The way you or your employees answer your phone, the way you respond to complaints from existing customers are just as important as advertisements, and press releases. Making you and your business look as good as possible at all times is at the core of a good marketing philosophy.

The Purpose and Ethics of Marketing

It is interesting that non-marketing people seem to think that marketing is manipulation and that because of this it is unethical or somehow compromising of one's ideals and principles. Only one point is correct; marketing does manipulate. In order to be of any use at all, marketing efforts – sales, advertising and public relations - have to inspire or motivate the consumer to phone you or come to your place of business. But, manipulating prospective clients with good marketing campaigns is not a matter of selling out, or compromising your ideals or principles and, as long as you are not attempting to commit fraud, there is nothing unethical about an effective marketing campaign. To my thinking the only bad marketing campaign is one that doesn't work or that is based on lies.

Marketing campaigns, advertising, public relations and other promotions are not intrinsically bad. However, for some odd reason, many people tend to look down on them, relying instead on word of mouth because they feel somehow that this is the more noble approach. These folks remind me a lot of college writing and art professors who preach incessantly that "one must suffer for their art", that to be a commercial success is a vile thing to be spurned at all costs. The origin of this idea is a mystery, but I suspect it may very well have been started by an instructor who turned to teaching because he couldn't make it commercially as a writer or artist. The idea caught on because there are far more unsuccessful artists, writers, poets and riding instructors or clinicians than there are successful ones. If a person happens to fall into the unsuccessful category, he can always find consolation with the idea that at least he "didn't sell out" by resorting to commercial marketing. To further cushion the sting of failure, the followers of the church-of-financial-success-only-comes-to-those-who-resort-to-the-evils-of-marketing there is the added belief that suffering is somehow romantic and spiritually edifying.

This is complete and utter baloney. The greatest writers of all time, Shakespeare, Tennyson, Lord Byron, Charlotte Bronte, Jane Austin, Charles Dickens, Mark Twain to name a few all enjoyed commercial success in their lifetime. Were they talented? Yes. Did word of mouth alone make them successful? No. Did they use the advertising and marketing options of the day to promote themselves? Absolutely.

Like the successful writers of the past, George Moore, Ian Miller, John Lyons, Monty Roberts, Nelson Passoa, Hilda Gurney and other great horsemen and women have also managed to achieve professional and financial success, and they have done so thanks to having the winning combination of talent in their profession and an understanding of effective marketing.

Talent

+

Good Marketing

=

Success

A GREAT DEMONSTRATION OF EFFECTIVE MARKETING

Not too long ago I was presenting a marketing workshop at a seminar for riding instructors. One of the other presenters was a wonderful clinician who is on a mission to improve the quality of riding instructors for the benefit of horses, riders and the instructors. As part of her presentation on building relationships, she brought a few very green horses into a round pen and proceeded to train them to come to her to be haltered.

She was patient, and persistent at making it more difficult for the horses to ignore her than it was for the horses to do what she wanted. She said that the first thing you had to work on was getting the horse to pay attention to you but not be frightened. Once you got that attention and the horse understood what was expected, he would eventually do what you wanted. It took some time and effort, but she accomplished her goal.

As I was watching this presentation, I thought it was one of the best examples of good marketing practices I had ever seen. She walked into the round pen with a clearly defined target market, and goals. She tailored her message to fit her particular market segment - green horses, an audience she understood well enough to know that it was quite different from horses that were haltered on a regular basis. She began by getting her market segment (the green horses) to pay attention to her - to notice her instead of the competition (the crowd of instructors who were watching the proceedings, the other horses and the guy in the nearby field who was cutting grass). Once she had the horses' attention, she gave them messages that were meaningful to them. She made it more difficult for them to do what they wanted than it was for them to do what she wanted. And, she didn't quit until she got the response she wanted, a response she decided on long before she even stepped into the horses' line of vision. In other words, she set the goal for her business, identified the market she was going to provide the service too, used information she had gathered through a lengthy study of this particular market, tailored her message and the medium for that message to suit this particular market's interests. She made certain that her message was one that appealed to her markets emotional needs, and she got them to pay more attention to her than all the other things in the area (the competition).

Talent

+

No Marketing

=

Failure

As any horse trainer can tell you, she would not have had to do the same things in the same way if she had well-trained horses in the round pen instead of very green horses. With trained horses her message and her medium would have been tailored differently so that she was doing what is necessary to get trained horses to do the same thing she wanted from the green horses. She would have still had to deal with all the competition for their attention, but what she had to do to get that attention, and the messages she gave them to communicate her goal and get them cooperate would certainly have been tailored specifically for them. Ultimately, regardless of training she would still have given the horses a reason to do what she was asking by making sure that she appealed to the emotional nature of the animal.

Every step was exactly what a good marketing professional does, and what you should do with your own business. Set your goals. Determine your audience. Shape your actions and your marketing to fit that audience. Make sure that you make it easier for them to do what you want than it is not to do it. Communicate with them on an emotional level, and you to will have them doing what you want.

Be forewarned however, that no marketing efforts, not even the best marketing in history can build long-term business or customer loyalty if the product or services you are selling are not of value to the customer or if you do not appreciate the customer properly. If the horses in the above example had felt unappreciated, if they felt threatened or uncomfortable, if the clinician had not known what she was doing, or if she had been uncertain about her goal, she would never had gotten the horses to cooperate and to help her reach her goal.

Further, if you do not believe that what you are selling, be it lessons, boarding, training, horses or horse shoeing or any other equine related product or service is of value, that it is better than what the competition is offering, then you have only two options- make what you are selling better than the competition or get out of business. If you decide you want to stay in business then go with the first option – make it better and market the day lights out of it.

Identifying Your Product or Service

Most people in the horse industry don't understand that, regardless of their occupation, they are selling a product. Aside from horses, tack, feed and medical supplies most of what is sold in the horse industry is less tangible; i.e. lessons, training, board, etc. but they are still "products" none the less.

To identify what you are selling, list the top 5 income generators for your horse business; i.e. group lessons, private lessons, group trail rides, custom trail rides, partial board, full board etc. You will need to determine not only which ones bring in the most revenue but also which ones are generating the greatest percentage of profit.

For example: Full board may bring in $45,000 per year, but when you subtract the cost of supplying board - property, insurance, stable hands, water, utilities, feed and hay, farm equipment, etc. you may find that you are actually losing money or that you are realizing a profit of only 5% of your total board cost. On the other hand you may discover that while your group lesson program generates only $20,000 a year your cost for supplying instruction for riders on their own horses is such that you are realizing a profit percentage of 55% or better. In such a case you would list your group lesson program as the first product you are "selling."

Use the information that you itemized in - *Determining Your Income* to help form a better idea of what you are "selling." on page xvi of the Appendix.

However, the key to selling more (getting the customer to buy more) is to understand what it is your customer is really "buying."

Who Are Your Customers?

It may be difficult to believe, but a good number of people in business make a lot of decisions based on assumptions, not on facts. One of the most common assumptions is where the majority of their profit is derived. The second most common assumption is in profiling their customers. Having an accurate profile of your real customer is valuable, because it determines everything from what colors and font you use in your logo to what to say in your ads and where to place them, as well as additional services you can offer to increase your income. Just like the clinician trying to halter green horses, everything she did from the type of halter and lead to the way she held it and approached the horse, everything you do in trying to market your business must be tailored specifically so that your particular customers will be most likely to respond to you in the way you want.

Don't confuse your actual customers with your target market. While you would hope they are the same, many existing businesses that have never established a target market and even some who do, often missed the mark or misjudged their market. Quite often existing businesses have no clear picture of who their customers actually are.

The narrower your scope, the more specific you can be about what you offer and to whom, the better.

If you ask the owner of a large boarding facility who his customers are you will usually get a very different answer than you will by asking the barn manager, or the riding instructors. The reason for this is that most people tend to assume that the customer is just like them or that the people they come into contact with on a regular basis are representative of the entire customer base. Because of these human tendencies the only way to get a real idea of who your customers are is to conduct a survey.

Surveys can be developed to help you discover the age and sex of the majority of your customers, the services they most often use and other such data that you can use to determine how to shape your business. For example if your survey indicates that the majority of your customers are beginning riders 8-12 years of age who attend only a few shows each year, you will want to develop ads that highlight that you specialize in beginning young riders and place the ads in publications aimed at parents of children in this age group or during cable television shows aimed at 8-12 year olds. You may also decide to expand your business into older intermediate riders who show more often. You would then tailor your advertising to reflect this goal by billing yourself as a Show Barn or the lesson program for Beginning and Intermediate riders.

Again, remember not to make the mistake of trying to be all things to all people. The narrower your scope, the more specific you can be about what you offer and to whom, the better.

To conduct your survey, you don't necessarily have to have each of your customers participate. You can simply use records from the last 12 - 24 months and the in-put of all of your employees. However, having your clients participate can provide you a means of determining new services to offer.

> **Sample Customer Survey** on pages xii of the Appendix, will give you an idea of how to create a survey for your particular business. You can create your own survey form or adapt the form in this book to suit your individual needs. *When developing your survey, you need to have a clear idea of what areas of your business you want to know more about. Generally, when profiling you want to know age, education, and income levels as well as the services your customers use and how they rate them.*
>
> *After you complete your survey fill out the Identifying Your Audience form on page xviii of the Appendix.*

Once you know which services your customers are using and consider important, it is time to consider what they are actually buying. While this may seem like an incredibly strange statement, the truth is what you think you are selling and what your customers are actually buying are rarely the same thing. You might wonder at how this is possible, after all, you have a lesson barn, your survey shows that the majority of your customers are taking lessons so they are obviously buying the lessons you are selling. You would be absolutely correct if it weren't for the fact that while your customers may appear to be buying things such as riding lessons, or horses, or shows, or whatever, they are actually buying intangible items that meet an emotional need. If you understand what the emotional need that your customers are actually trying to fill by buying your goods or services, you will be able to win more customers and build stronger customer loyalty, both of which will increase the amount of money you can make with your horse business.

For example: You have a lesson barn. The majority of your students are girls from 12 – 16 years of age who take at least one lesson per week. At first glance you might expect that the reason behind this purchase is that the girls are trying to build skills. But why are they choosing riding over some other sport or activity? What emotional need is riding fulfilling? Is it the same need as the parent who is paying for the lessons? Why is this information even important?

Logic vs. Emotion - Which one do you appeal to?

Most people assume that decisions to purchase are based entirely on logic or at least 75% logic- 25% emotion. They base their marketing strategies on convincing the customer that their service or product is better made, a better value, longer lasting and on and on. They are wrong. The reality is that consumers use logic to justify their decision, but emotion is the real controlling factor in every decision to purchase. No matter how much we humans try to deny it, emotions are the driving force in almost everything we do.

If this were not true, Mercedes would never sell their cars, Rolex would never sell against Timex and on and on. True, for some people, price is the driving factor but even that is based on an emotional decision.

Scientific studies have repeatedly proven that every human has two reasons for doing anything - the rational reason and the emotional reason. The rational reason is generally based on what the person can claim to be based on intellectual and/or informed reasons. The emotional reason is exactly that - based on emotions such as love, affection, the desire to be thought well of, etc. In EVERY instance the EMOTIONAL REASON is the real reason humans commit an action. There are many theories and explanations for this, most particularly a connection to the primitive core of the human brain known as the amygdela.

In EVERY instance the EMOTIONAL REASON is the real reason humans commit an action.

While the workings of the human brain make for some fascinating and useful reading, all you really need to know is that emotions are the key to a good marketing program. In order to win customers, you have to appeal to their emotions. To understand the emotional reasons for their horse related choices, you have to have a better understanding of your customers.

The emotional reason behind a customer's decision to purchase a carriage ride is quite different from the emotional reasons that drive a 25 year old riding student to purchase riding lessons and even more different from the emotional reasons parents choose a given trainer or riding instructor or boarding facility over another. Until you understand what the emotional factor is, you will have difficulty developing a successful marketing program.

For example: You are a riding instructor who teaches hunter/jumpers or dressage. Your clientele consists of two groups of females, one ages 8 - 16 and the other ages 25 - 45. The latter group tends to choose trainers based on the relationship they can establish with the trainer - they have to LIKE you. In such a case, your marketing approach should be to sell how approachable and sociable you are. When potential customers call or come to your stable you need to take lots of time getting to know them and letting them get to know you.

The younger group, females 8 – 16, is a lot trickier because the parent, not the student ultimately makes the decision. Generally speaking there are two types of parents, those who come from a horse background and those who do not. Those parents, who come from a horse background, will most often choose a trainer based on expertise and results. Safety and knowledge are critical as these parents are informed consumers, they know the dangers and risks involved in riding and they can usually tell if the trainer knows what he is doing. To appeal to this parent, you will need to emphasize your training, expertise and safety in your marketing.

Those parents who lack previous horse experience generally have no idea how to tell a good trainer from a bad one. These two parent groups can be broken down further into several sub-groups:

1. Those who support their child's desire to ride because it matters to the child

2. Those who encourage the child's riding because the parent(s) are living vicariously through their child and fulfilling their own life-long dream of horsemanship,

3. Those who simply want to impress their friends.

The first group is most likely to choose a trainer based on convenience, price and the child's reaction to the trainer.

The second group is most likely to choose a trainer based on how closely the facility, the lesson horses and the trainer fit the image of their dream. They are also more influenced by how well the trainer interacts with them.

For the third group, the status of having a child who rides plays a key role in demonstrating the parents' level of wealth whether that wealth is real or imagined. In such cases the parent will choose not the most qualified trainer but the one who is most socially acceptable to the parents' friends - they are not paying for lessons; they are paying for bragging rights. To appeal to these parents, you need to have either - a local celebrity or a list of several socially prominent customers, an impressive resume of national and/or international competition, and/or a very posh facility in a great location. More importantly you need to make these items the focus of your marketing.

The more you are able to convince customers that you can satisfy their primitive needs, the more successful you will be.

The thing to remember is that, no matter how practical and logical people pretend to be, humans are overwhelmingly controlled by very primitive instincts. The more you able to convince customers that you can satisfy those primitive needs, the more successful you will be. The best way to do this is not to focus on the features of your business such as the number of horses, stalls and wash racks you have, or your qualifications, or how you do what you do. Focus on the results or benefits the customer can expect and tie them to the basic human needs. How will your services make them smarter, wealthier, prettier, more popular, thinner, more respected, etc.? Figure that out and use it.

This should be fairly easy if you have really worked out what you are offering and the people you want to offer it to, and have a clear profile of your customers. Once you know the emotional reason behind the purchase or what the customer is actually buying you have to incorporate it into everything you do to market your business. Ultimately, the emotional need you fill is the only thing that really matters to your customer; it is your chief BENEFIT.

Benefit VS Feature

Quite often business people confuse benefits with features. **Benefits** are the aspect of your business that fulfills an emotional need - it tells the customer what is in it for them. **Benefits** are *why* you do the things you do. **Features** are the aspects of your business that lead to the benefit, *how* you provide the benefit. This can be very confusing but, it may help you if you think in terms of benefits being abstract and features being tangibles.

For example: A farrier may offer hot and cold shoeing, custom shoes, specialize in therapeutic shoeing, offer special types of shoes that no one else does. These are all features – they are the types of shoes and shoeing techniques. They are not benefits and should not be used in marketing your business. But hot shoeing is a big deal you might say. Okay, why? *What benefit does it offer my horse or me? How will it improve my life?* It gives more options to assure a better fitting shoe? *So what?* Well a better fitting shoe will keep your horse sound, saving money on vet bills and give you more time in the saddle. *Ahhhh! Now that matters.* Keeping my horse sound will save me money, and allow me more time doing something I enjoy, like riding. You've just told me that you can make me wealthier and happier so, I am more likely to pay attention to what you are saying and to respond by calling you to set up an appointment if you tell me *John Doe Shoeing, will help keep your horse sound with shoes guaranteed to fit your horse.* If instead you tell me *John Doe Shoeing, hot and cold shoeing, therapeutic shoeing and alumni and rubber shoes* you are leaving it up to me to figure out why that matters and if it matters enough.

If you have a **boarding barn**, don't let the facility take center stage, put the spotlight on the benefit. In other words, don't tell me that you have 6 turnout pastures,

135 acres of riding trails, and 100 stall boarding barn. All of those sound fine, but you would be more likely to see customers respond if you let statements such as – *We spoil our horses with lavish attention and personal care*, or *We do all the work so you can have all the fun of owning a horse* take the spotlight in your ads, flyers, brochures and other marketing materials. If you want to include the features of your facility, fine, as long as you have the room to do so without making things crowded or difficult to read.

If you work in equine assisted psychotherapy, don't tell me that you offer counseling and the various kinds of sessions or plans tell me -*We create happy families*, or Got *a teenager that's driving you nuts? We can help.*

And don't tell me about the details of your tack shop. Tell me *be the envy of everyone at the next horse show on and off your horse.*

It is critically important that you figure out the greatest benefits you offer customers and state them clearly in your marketing materials.

Always keep in mind that human beings are relatively lazy, particularly when it comes to responding to marketing materials. They don't want to have to work hard to figure out what benefits you offer. What's more, you can't always guarantee that when left to figure it out for themselves - customers rarely see the benefits you offer them unless you point them out. It is therefore critically important that you figure out the greatest benefits you offer customers and state them clearly in your marketing materials. Don't leave it to chance or you may miss out on a lot of new customers or fail to keep existing ones.

The ***Benefits Your Business Offers Potential Clients, The Three Most Meaningful, Exciting and/or Fun Reasons for Doing Business with You and Your Most Important Benefit and Where to Use It*** forms on pages xix of the Appendix may help you with this.

BENEFIT vs FEATURE

Benefit: what the customer ultimately wants to gain from a product or service.

Feature: a device or modification that provides a benefit.

Feature	Benefit
Gelding	Consistant Temperment
Quality Instruction	More Ribbons (Safer)
Trainer with Elite Clientele	More Prestige

Chapter Six

Marketing Communications

Marketing communications are all the techniques a business uses to get their message out to their potential and existing customers. Marketing communications may include: advertisements, billboards, brochures, newsletters, post cards, printed menus, web sites, flyers, business cards, signs, press releases, magazine articles, news coverage, the sides of your truck and horse trailer, tack stall curtains, and so on and so forth. While the forms of communicating with customers are quite varied, the goal of all such communications is to entice potential customers to contact you when they need a product or service that you offer, or keep existing customers spending money with you.

From this point forward you need to consider everything you say and do as part of your marketing communications. Earlier we covered your vision of yourself and how that effects how others see you. Now is the time to put that vision to work for you and make sure you are not inadvertently undermining your marketing efforts.

If your vision is to be a boarding facility with the best care possible, you had better make sure your facility looks like the best. While this doesn't mean you have to have the most expensive or posh facility in the area, it does mean that the stalls have to be spotless, the horses clean and healthy looking, and your boarders content. If all of this is not reflecting that you actually are living up to your marketing materials, you won't build the kind of business you want. So begin living up to your self-image. If your image of your professional self isn't reflecting the level of quality you are promising, fix it.

Any time you are with a client or around potential clients, your behavior is your best or worst advertisement. If you have shown in any discipline, then you know that during the late or early schooling times, when few parents are around, there are trainers and instructors who scream and curse at their students, some to the point of emotional abuse. To get away with this kind of behavior, you have to be either the best trainer around or specialize in teaching masochists. There are four trainers in my area who have students who win like crazy, and I wouldn't have put my child or her horse in the hands of any one of them, even if they were the only choices in town. I feel this way because of the things I heard them say to their students when they didn't think anyone was listening. So be careful what you say, and learn to control your stress and anger in ways that are less damaging to your students, your horses and, ultimately, yourself. From this point on realize that you are **always** advertising your business whether you intend to or not, and there are always people watching and listening.

Communicating Effectively

For most people, communicating means talking. The first form of communication any human has with another is spoken. Mothers and fathers talk to their infants and the child eventually talks back, sometimes to their own detriment but that is another issue. Research shows that humans remember what they hear more easily than things they see or read. This preference for using spoken words to communicate instead of written ones adds to the challenge of developing effective marketing communications. You, the writer, don't particularly like to write, and the reader is less likely to remember what he reads. To overcome these two obstacles there are a few tricks that will help.

Copy Writing Formula for Success

First of all use simple words and sentence structure. For most of us, the majority of writing we have done has been for either a class we were taking or an academic thesis. In both of these instances, the writing was done primarily to please and/or impress a teacher. The techniques used are not suitable for marketing, because writing for marketing is all about communication – period! Grammar and an impressive vocabulary must take a back seat here and leave communication in the driver's seat.

Numerous studies have been conducted that clearly demonstrate a few basic rules for effective communication. The results show that the fewer syllables per word, the fewer words per sentence, the fewer sentences per paragraph, the fewer paragraphs per page, the more effective your message will be. When writing to communicate, the KISS (Keep It Simple Stupid) rule applies.

Keep the language readable. Avoid using clinical terms and semantics that are not easily understood by the general public. Look for easier, shorter versions of a word or expression. Never use a big word when a little one will do.

	Impressive	Easier	Easier still	Easiest
For example:	Instantaneously >	instantly >	quickly >	fast

Avoid using insider terms or jargon. Terms like "on the bit," "ahead of the motion," "missing the spot," are all fine and good in a lesson where you are trying to teach the terms commonly

*You are_*
always
*advertising your business whether you intend to or not, and there are **always** people watching and listening.*

used in a given discipline, or if you want to impress people by making them think you know more than they do. But when you are trying to communicate with potential customers, who may or may not have a clue about the meaning of such terms, such jargon can be disastrous. For customers to want to do business with you, they must have a clue as to what you are offering them and they must feel that they are on equal footing intellectually. No one likes to feel stupid or confused. If you make them feel either way, they are not going to turn to you when they need what you are selling.

Forget everything your English teachers have taught you and address your reader as "you." It keeps the message personal and directed to the reader and his needs. Focus on his needs and how you can meet them better than anyone else can. And, be sure you don't come across as talking down to the reader. It is a tough balance to reach but when you do, your message will come across loud and clear and get real results.

Don't use humor. Humor can be great but it is extremely difficult to write because so much of humor relies on how something is said more than the words themselves. With written humor you run the risk of being misunderstood or the reader being insulted. Neither of which is going to win you customers.

Get to the point. If you waste time beating around the bush, trying to warm up before you tell the reader what's in it for them, you will lose their interest. Like a good military special forces attack, your goal in writing for marketing purposes is to get in, get the job done, and get out as fast as you can making sure that you don't leave any potential customers behind to fall into the enemy's (competition's) hands. And don't over explain. All the customer needs to know is what they are going to get out of their association with you, and information that backs it up.

Use active verbs in the present tense, i.e. *Learn, Change, Grow, Solve, Win.* Avoid *"will be able to,"* or *"may be able to"* or verbs that end with "ing." Get directly to the action. When it comes to writing effective copy that sells, focus on the benefit you offer and describe it with as many active verbs as possible. At the end remember to always ask for the action you want most – "Call today!" "Call Now!" And don't forget to include your phone number

Realize that writing is a process; even professionals don't get it right the first time. Follow the method that professional writers use – write ten times the amount of text you need then cut it down to the bones, so that all that remains are the most important points you want to make. Just make sure that those

Your goal in writing for marketing purposes is to get in, get the job done, and get out as fast as you can making sure that you don't leave any potential customers behind to fall into the competition's hands.

points support your benefit and don't bore the reader with lots of needless details about how you do things.

Marketing Communication Guidelines:

❖ Focus on the Benefit.

❖ Always be honest.

❖ Keep the language simple.

❖ Dazzle customers with substance, not B.S.

❖ Be brief and to the point.

❖ Put yourself in the customer's shoes, know what is important to them and make sure it is as important to you.

Call to Action

You have spent all this time learning that to sell your business, to win new customers you must tell the benefits of your service, yet it will all be for nothing if you don't ask the reader to take action. Every marketing piece you create must end with a call to action.

Great calls to action include:

❖ Call today.

❖ Drop by today.

❖ Call today, start living better tomorrow.

❖ Take action - call now.

❖ Don't waste another day stopping at fences. Call us.

The list is endless. Just remember to keep it simple and active. You want them to do something and you want them to do it now. And to help them be able to take action you must include the critical detail – **YOUR CONTACT INFORMATION**.

I am constantly amazed by business owners who fail to include their phone number and e-mail or web site address on all of their materials. It should be on everything to do with your business including tack stall curtains.

Make It Easy

When you put together your materials make certain that it is easier for the customer to do what you want (spend money with you) than it is for her to do something else (not spend money with you). Make sure that what it is you want them to do is very clear. Call today or come by to visit, schedule an appointment or lesson. If it is to call make the phone number easy to find. Include several phone numbers if necessary. If you want the customer to come to your business, include directions and a map with specific instructions. If you want the customer to register for a horse show, make certain that the forms and instructions are easy to use and understand for someone who may never have seen such a form before.

People will avoid situations that make them feel embarrassed or stupid. Do what ever you can to prevent them from associating you with such negative feelings.

It doesn't matter how great your benefit and call to action are; if you don't include your phone number, no one is going to call. Human beings are inherently lazy and are not about to take the time to look up a phone number. So make sure you include your phone number, the hours you are available, your address and, if you have the room, a small map with directions on how to get to your place of business.

Positives and Negatives

Every business has positives and negatives. In all of your marketing communications materials, it is important that you play up your positives, but don't ignore the negatives. Sometimes the negatives can be transformed into positives.

For example: You have the smallest barn in town. This means that you don't have a lot of turn out, or lots of stalls, or a covered arena like your competition, but what you lack in size you make up for in personal service that the big barns can't match. In your marketing materials, you would be wise not to play down your small size, but to play it up by saying something like-*XYZ Stables, the small barn with the best service in three counties.*

In all of your marketing materials, it is important that you play up your positives, but don't ignore the negatives.

If you offer a service or goods that are similar to others in your area, try to find a means of making yourself more unique. If you have a tack shop in an area where there is stiff competition, then one of the services you may want to offer is free barn delivery. If you do acupuncture, therapeutic message, or dentistry and going to your clients' barns or stables is one of the services you offer, make sure you put that information in bold type near your phone number. It is a strong selling point. Make certain you emphasize these extras even if everyone in the business offers the same service. Lots of businesses assume that every customer knows that an equine message therapist does barn calls and don't include this information in their marketing materials. What do you think happens when potential customers go through several equine message therapists' ads or brochures that don't have this information then come across one that plainly states, we come to your barn, at your convenience? Guess which massage therapist gets the most calls.

Fonts

When using different fonts for logos, ads, or other marketing materials there are a few rules you need to be aware of. There are three basic styles of font – serif, san serif and decorative (also know as display). Serif fonts have little lines (serifs) at the ends of the strokes that form the letters. These serifs actually help the eye move along a line of text. This is why serif fonts are preferred for lengthy blocks of text including magazine articles and books. San serif fonts do not have these additional strokes. They are without (san) serifs. San serif fonts are like modern architecture – spare and unadorned. Decorative fonts can be either serif or san serif but they are so decorative that they are not easily read. This makes decorative fonts ideal for headlines and short lines of type. Decorative fonts are not suitable for body copy or large blocks of text because they require the eye to do more work.

Serif	San Serif	Decorative
Bookman Old Style	Arial	Art Deco
Caslon Light	Comic Sans	BERTRAM
Century Schoolbook	Enviro	Caslon Open
Footlight	Franklin Gothic	Disobey
Garamond	Haettenschweiler	Jokerman
Keyboard	Lucida Sans	Mistral
Times New Roman	Univers	Viva

Readability is ALWAYS more important than Decoration.

Font Guidelines:

❖ Choose fonts based on your target market audience and the feelings the fonts evoke. DO NOT choose fonts simply because you may *like* them.

❖ Most women prefer thin more decorative fonts.

❖ Most Men prefer thick san serif fonts.

❖ Serif fonts are better for large blocks of text than san serif fonts.

❖ Never combine more than two fonts in an ad or logo.

❖ Never use the same fonts that are in your logo for anything else on a business card, ad or brochure, etc. It will make your logo less noticeable.

❖ When using two fonts together, combine serif and san serif, or decorative and serif, or decorative and san serif fonts.

❖ For contrast use fonts of different thicknesses. If you use a thin serif font for the company name, use a fat san serif font for a tag line or vice versa.

❖ Use a single font for body copy and headlines but use boldness, italics or different font sizes for variety.

❖ Italic and script fonts tend to have more motion than non-italic and script. Italic fonts that lean to the right evoke feelings of optimism and positive action while fonts that lean to the left evoke feelings of pessimism and defensiveness.

❖ READABILITY IS ALWAYS MORE IMPORTANT THAN DECORATION.

Colors

You may not have ever given color much thought in the past, but the impact of color on the effectiveness of your marketing materials is important enough for you to learn a few basics. All colors evoke emotional response that can work for you or against you. Strong, bright colors appear more energetic, dark colors are more imposing or heavy, pastels are lightweight, more passive, neutral shades feel exactly that - neutral, not evoking any emotion at all.

Red is energetic. It represents excitement, strength, sex, passion, speed, and danger. It also stimulates creativity.

Blue is the most popular color and signifies trust, reliability, belonging, and coolness. Tests have shown that people are more productive in blue rooms.

Yellow is the color of the sun and is associated with warmth, sunshine, cheerfulness, and happiness. While softer shades of yellow enhance concentration, bright yellow is difficult for the human eye to take and needs to be used judiciously.

Orange is also an emotionally warming color that is mentally associated with playfulness, warmth, and vibrancy

Green is the color of nature. It gives off feelings of freshness and is associated with growth, and abundance. Green can actually improve vision.

Purple is a tricky color. While it is associated with royal, spirituality, dignity and sophistication it is rare in nature and can easily appear artificial, which may make purple an unwise choice for EAP businesses.

Pink is the color of softness, sweetness, and security.

White is the color of purity. It is clean, youthful, and mild. It is also so common that marketing materials that are predominantly white tend to go unnoticed.

Black is strong, the color of authority. It is sophisticated, elegant, seductive, and mysterious.

Gold, particularly metallic gold is linked with the precious metal. It represents prestige and a high price tag.

Silver is more cold than gold, and is more closely linked with scientific precision.

Brown is the color of the earth. It is the color of reliability. Light brown is associated with sincerity, genuineness.

When using color in your marketing materials try to pick out those that most appeal to your particular audience.

For example: If you have a lesson barn and your customers are primarily children, the parent is the real buyer. So while children like bright, bold colors, the parents may be buying safety and might react better to brown or blue or a combination of the two. If your customers are more the socially competitive types then blacks, metallic gold and green might work really well for you.

❖ When using color in your logo or sign, use the opposite colors of your strongest competitors. If they are using green and beige, you should use red and white or yellow, or navy and gray. The idea is to look different from the competition.

❖ As a rule women lean towards pastel colors while men prefer dark conservative colors. However, in the world of hunter/jumper and dressage riders, the females tend to prefer the more masculine colors of brown, navy and hunter green.

❖ Strong colors work best for lettering and light colors for background.

❖ **Warning:** As a rule dark letters on a dark background are difficult to read. Large areas of dark background with light type can also be difficult to read if the colors are different shades of the same color family.

Pictures and Clipart

A big mistake horse people typically make is in using the same or similar clip art to that used by their competitors. There are thousands of clipart disks with hundreds of thousands of pictures of horses and horse related items such as horse shoes, crops, French horns, boots, etc. Make certain that whatever you use is very different from all of the equine vets, trainers, stables, shows, rodeos, tack stores and other horse related businesses in you area. You don't want to spend time and money promoting them, which is exactly what you will be doing if the customer confuses your logo with your competitors'.

One Size Doesn't Fit All

Another big mistake businesses make is to try to "sell" or present more than one service or product with a single marketing piece.

Another big mistake I see businesses make is to try to "sell" or present more than one service or product with a single marketing piece. If a business offers lessons and boarding, if they sell products to Western and English clients, if they do EAP counseling and corporate training, they want to include them all in the same brochure, flyer, ad, etc. They feel that by doing things this way they will SAVE MONEY by only having to pay for one piece.

While one piece is less expensive than two, is it really less expensive if that one piece is designed to go after more than one target market at a time and ends up appealing to none? Almost without exception every target market has a different need, a different benefit that will appeal to them. If you are looking for a place to board your horse, do you care about how many riding lesson a barn offers, or do you care about the quality of horse care? If you are buying English tack, do you care that the store offers Western Tack? Of course you don't.

In addition to different target markets responding to different benefits, trying to promote more than one thing at a time sends the message that you may be okay in both but you are an expert in neither, and therefore, they are less likely to respond positively to your marketing piece. Expertise sells and it is difficult to present yourself as an expert in many areas even if you are. Your marketing will be more effective if you generate separate marketing materials for each of your areas of expertise.

Marketing pieces do not have the room to effectively promote anything that is not aimed at a very specific target market audience. The more general you try to be, the more markets you try to incorporate or appeal to, the less effective your pieces will be.

While you may think that because a brochure is larger than an ad, with three separate panels, you can get away with trying to appeal to three different markets. This is a mistake. If you are trying to save money, it is better to create three separate 3 2/3" by 8 ½" brochures that are each promoting one service to one market, than to create one 11" by 8 ½" three panel brochure promoting three separate services aimed at three different markets. And it won't cost you that much more to do it.

There is a sample of an 11"x 8 ½" page set up as three separate one panel brochures xxvii -xxix, each aimed at a different audience on page of the Appendix.

For example: I have a client who owns a facility that conducts a wide variety of horsemanship clinics each year. He also has cabins and lodging available on the site that are appealing to non-horse owners as well as the horse owners who attend his clinics. While he has no problem understanding that each clinic has to be promoted separately, he has a tough time understanding that he must promote the lodging and the clinics separately. He doesn't understand that to keep his lodging filled, he needs to appeal to a larger audience than horse owners. These non-horse people will not be interest in vacationing at a facility that has horsemanship clinics. It is not a selling point to them and may only confuse them into thinking that they must ride or own a horse to stay at the lodge.

Testimonials

Nothing sells like a satisfied customer, so put your happy customers to work for you. Have them write up testimonials that you can use in all of your marketing materials. These testimonials need to sound as if they were written by real people, so resist the urge to change them beyond correcting spelling and grammatical errors or

It is better to create three separate 3 2/3" by 8 ½" brochures that are each promoting one service to one market, than to create one 11" by 8 ½" three panel brochure promoting three separate services aimed at three different markets.

shortening them. Testimonials have more credibility if they include the customer's full name. Do not use the customer's address, or other contact, or personal information except for competition titles such as "2003 IDA National Individual Champion Upper Training Level."

Professional Titles and Designations

If you have special training, or professional designations that you have earned, you should definitely include them in your marketing materials as they support your ability to actually provide the benefit you are telling customers that you will provide. However, avoid the temptation to use a string of initials after your name. Most of these initials are a mystery to anyone who is not a professional in the same field or segment of the horse industry. Such things as CEP, MSW, LFC, or ARIA CLIHS after a name may mean something to someone with similar designations but most customers won't have a clue. They will be much more impressed if you write out – Certified Equine Practitioner, Master Social Work, Licensed Family Counselor, and American Riding Instructors Association Certified Level I Hunt Seat. If you don't have the room to write them all out, use fewer or consider dropping them all together. You can always give customers a copy of your resume when they come to see you for the first time.

Testing Your Materials

The best way to make sure that you don't waste your money on marketing materials that don't work is to test them in advance.

The best way to make sure that you don't waste your money on marketing materials that don't work is to test them in advance. You may have heard about "focus groups" used by manufacturers and for years.

Focus groups are made up of people who are asked to review goods or services before they are released to the general public. Ideally focus groups match the demographics of the company's target market audience. Toy manufacturer's use children, soft drink manufacturers will use all ages, retirement communities will use people over 50.

Focus groups have been used for decades. The problem is that recent research indicates that focus groups are useless because when you ask people –"What do you like about this? What do you dislike about that? Etc. They almost always tell you what they think you want to hear, or don't want to hear, depending on their personality. So then, how do you test ads, brochures and other expensive marketing materials to see if they are going to work before you spend your limited marketing dollars? I recommend that, once you have the piece the way you think it should be, print out hard copy. Take this print out, along with several other similar pieces from other businesses, preferably your competition, and spread them all on a table at your barn or place of business at a time when you will have people there. Don't point the materials out to anyone; don't ask any questions, just as inconspicuously as possible stand back and watch.

When people walk up to the table, which piece do they pick up first? Which ones do they actually read? Which one do they put in their pocket or ask if they can have?

Keep a tally of these reactions. If the brochure, ad or flyer that is most often picked up first isn't yours, take a good hard look at it, comparing it to yours. What is different about it? Is it the colors, fonts, layout, or message? Then try to incorporate those things into your piece. Keep testing until your marketing piece is the one that is picked up and read.

Keep in mind that for this testing process to be most effective, you cannot tell anyone what you are doing or why. You also need to test it with different groups. If you keep testing the same kind of marketing piece with the same folks day after day, they are going to catch on and you won't get true responses.

With print ads, it is a good idea to generate a print out on the same kind of paper that the publication you plan to run it in uses. Make sure that, if the ad will run in black and white, you don't print it out in color and vice versa. Trim the ad down to size and paste it in place over a similar size in the actual publication you plan to advertise in. Then set this publication out for people to find for themselves. Let their reactions help you decide on what changes, if any, that you need to make.

Whatever you do, don't ask people what they "think" about your marketing materials. Thinking is a rational process, reacting is an emotional process and as was pointed out earlier, the emotional process is the one you need to tap into. The only way to see if you are doing that successfully is to present the materials as described above or put them out into the public and wait for a response.

Keep in mind that even if people "think" your marketing piece is bad, it doesn't mean that it won't work effectively.

In marketing, what people "think" about your materials aren't as important as how they "react" to them.

An Effective Marketing Campaign that Customers Hated

I once had a client who created a tool. You couldn't tell what it did by looking at it. In fact the image might cause a person to dismiss it. So instead, I relied on words to "show" the products benefit. You would not believe how many people would come up to us at trade shows just to get a look at this tool that they "couldn't even begin to picture in their heads" and of course to tell us how much they hated our ads because they drove them crazy with curiosity. Sure they hated my ad; it made them so curious that some of them spent hours trying to find us just so they could finally see this fantastic tool, inadvertently giving us the chance to sell them the tool. This would have never happened if I had used the photo as everyone including the man who created the tool "thought" we should do.

In marketing, what people "think" about your materials aren't as important as how they "react" to them.

Tracking

Once your ad, flyer, business card, newspaper article or any other form of advertising or public relations is in place for potential customers to see, the most important thing you can do is track the results. This is not a complicated process, takes very little time and can make a significant difference in how effective your marketing materials actually are. It will also save you thousands of dollars in the long run by keeping you from using media and messages that don't work for you.

To set up a tracking system, begin by purchasing a low-tech spiral notebook and attaching a pen or pencil to it. Place it beside every phone that you answer for business purposes. (This means you may have to purchase more than one.) Cut out your ad, and tape it to a page. Below it write the date the ad is running, the publication it is running in and the cost. For brochures, flyers, etc. tape them on one page, and use the facing page to write where they were placed or the date they were mailed, the number of pieces at this location and the cost for each piece.

Then anytime anyone calls or comes by your place of business ALWAYS ASK: How or where the caller or visitor heard of your business. Make a tally mark each time they answer "I saw your ad in ___, I got a copy of your brochure (flyer, prize list, etc) in the mail, I picked up one of your (brochures, flyers, prize lists, business cards, at ___ or I saw your name on a placemat at ___." Be sure to teach **_ALL_** of your employees (and family if they answer your business phone) to do the same.

This information will show you exactly how good a particular publication or location or marketing piece is at bringing customers to you for you to sell. It will also show you if you need to work on your phone or personal presentation. If the majority of callers or visitors who respond to your marketing materials are not becoming customers then you need to work on your sales ability, or make changes with your facility instead of changing your marketing materials.

The best marketing materials in the world won't sell your products or services. They will however bring the customer to you in person, over the phone or via the internet and give you the opportunity to sell your products or services.

> *You will find a sample tracking page setup on page xlv of the Appendix.*

Chapter Seven

Advertising

A dvertising is without a doubt one of the best ways to increase your income by increasing the number of customers buying your goods or services. However you need to know one important fact about advertising: ***Ads are not meant to sell your services or products; Ads are meant to excite customers to call, go to your web site, or come by your barn or business so that YOU can sell your service or products.***

The secrets to effective advertising are similar to those for all effective marketing, know your audience, know what they are buying, know how you stack up compared to the competition, know how to tailor your message so that it has real impact, and know how to choose the best place to put your message so that it has the best impact.

Beyond that you need to know what your advertising budget actually is. I fully understand that it is difficult for most horse businesses to find the money to spend on advertising. It is precisely because money for advertising is so scarce that it is vitally important for you to formulate a plan for spending every penny as effectively as possible. There are no hard, fast rules as to how much of your total operating budget you need to devote to advertising. There is a formula floating around that says you should dedicate 3% -5% of your anticipated gross to advertising. This means that, if you want to bring in $100,000 in total revenues during a year's time, you need to invest $3,000 to $5,000 on that year's advertising.

If you can spare that kind of cash for advertising, that is wonderful. If all you can afford is $10 a month that is okay, too. It may take you longer to build your business when you have a small budget, but no matter how large or small your advertising budget is, you need to have one and you need to know what to do to make sure that every dollar you spend brings results.

When you don't have a clear idea of what you can afford to spend, you can't determine the kinds of advertising you are going to do and schedule it to work for you. You also become very vulnerable to fast talking advertising sales reps.

Once you have determined what you are going to spend each year on advertising, I highly recommend that you carefully consider how you are going to spend it, and, once you have made your choices, stick with them. Once you place one ad in a newspaper, magazine, on the radio, television or billboard, ad representatives from every other medium in town are going to be calling on you trying to convince you that they are the perfect medium to place your ads. These folks mean well, but the truth is they make money selling ad space. Their sales commission may be much more important than your results. Trust me, in 30 plus years I have never once heard an ad sales rep tell me or any of my clients that their particular medium wouldn't work for them. That is why you have to know how much you can realistically afford to spend on advertising, decide in advance where you are going to place your ads, and stick with your plan. Of course you can make exceptions if you suddenly find you have more money to spend on advertising, or if one of one of more of the media you chose isn't bringing you results. In such cases you can run additional ads in the same medium, run in an additional medium or replace the media that haven't worked.

The Medium

At this point, you should know who your audience is, what they are buying and how you compare to your competition. You should have a firm understanding of your benefits and features. The trick now is to figure out how to tailor your message and find the best place to put it, which is also known as choosing the medium for your message. (Media is the plural for all available advertising outlets - magazines, television, cable and radio stations, billboards, newsletters, web sites etc. Medium is the singular form of the word and means a specific magazine, etc.)

Research has shown that a message that is seen and heard (TV or movies) is more likely to be remembered than that which is merely heard. Messages that are heard (radio) are more likely to be remembered than messages that are seen (print). Despite the fact that research indicates that television is the most likely to be remembered, the medium of choice for most horse businesses and non-horse businesses is print.

The reasons for this preference for print media are simple – print is generally the most affordable form of advertising, particularly flyers, business cards, and prize lists. Radio can be affordable, but radio campaigns tend to work best for event promotion, a large show, or clinic, or are having a big sale, etc. Radio is simply too expensive for most horse businesses. Television is even more expensive than radio.

Of course there is one effective and affordable television advertising for a horse business - the local weather channel. Everyone watches the weather channel and the banner ads – the line of words that runs across the bottom of the screen, are amazingly effective. Prices vary from city to city but a week of banner advertising on weather channels can run as little as $100 for 25-50 words. Ultimately, though, banner advertising is still printed advertising and has to be treated as such. The benefit message has to be the primary focus, each word has to be supportive of that benefit and you must have the correct contact information.

Most books on advertising devote a lot of space to the importance of choosing the proper medium for your message. I personally don't think it is that complicated. It is simply a matter of logic, an understanding that, if you want your ads or message to have the greatest impact, the smartest thing to do is put your ads or messages in places most likely to be seen by your potential customers.

If you offer western reigning lessons, would you put an ad in a magazine that features nothing but articles on hunter/jumpers? If you own an English tack shop, would you put up a flyer at a western barn? Would you see better results advertising in a horse related publication or one that has nothing to do with horses?

The benefit message has to be the primary focus, each word has to be supportive of that benefit.

The answers to each one of these seem obvious, but what do you do if you live in a community that doesn't have a horse related newspaper or magazine? And what about radio, or bulletin boards or the Internet? How do you decide where to advertise, or do you simply forget about advertising all together?

At the beginning of this book, I spoke about media kits and how to use them to determine how many potential customers that are interested in horses reside in a given area. The media kits that helped you determine the size of your market can also help you to determine whether or not you want to use a particular publication, television or radio station. That is the purpose for which they were designed in the first place. By looking at the demographics of the readers or viewers of each individual publication and electronic media outlet (TV, radio, cable, internet) you will get the best feel for how well a particular medium will work for you.

Since you already know the age, education, and income of your customers, all you have to do is look at the demographics of various media to determine which ones are the closest match to and offer the greatest number of your potential customers. From there you need to determine how much it is going to cost you to reach your potential customers on a per customer basis. The medium's total circulation number will help you calculate this cost per thousand.

For example: *Your research shows that a local horse magazine has a total circulation of 10,000. Their reader demographic profile indicates that 60% of their readers are the same age, education, income level, and riding discipline of the majority of your customers. This means that 6,000 of their readers will most likely to be interested in your goods or services. The cost for a reasonable size, ¼* *page, ad is $600. This means that you will pay $600 to put your message in front of 6,000 people who are likely to become your customers for a cost of $.10 each.*

If your local newspaper has a total circulation of 60,000 and their reader demographics shows that 10% of their readers are the same age, education and income level as your clients, and may or may not ride or have an interest in horses. Running a classified ad in this newspaper costs $150 each week. Any ad you place in this publication will reach 600 potential customers for a cost of $4 each. In this instance, even though the ad in the horse publication seems to be more expensive, you are actually paying far less per potential customer than you are by using a classified ad. Of course if you try the horse publication and you only get five phone calls, but a classified ad generates 25 to 50 calls, you might need to forget about the horse magazine.

The key to spending your advertising budget effectively is to constantly look for those outlets – newspapers, magazines, and other such media that have demographics as close to your customer profile as possible for the best price.

What to Do with a REALLY Small Budget

But what about a business that can't really afford regular advertising channels such as publications and radio? There are still lots of options. Bulletin boards are the perfect place for a great flyer or a business card and all it will cost you is the price of the piece you pin up. The key is to have a really nice card or flyer or brochure if space will allow, and to know which bulletin boards are going to be seen by your audience – feed stores, tack shops, grocery stores and public libraries are generally very good. If you are aiming for college students, then the bulletin board in student union or activity center is ideal. If your primary audience is female and/or children, don't overlook toy stores, day care centers and beauty salons or any other store frequented by women. If you primary customer is male, then car repair shops, sporting goods stores and barbershops are good places to post your advertising message. If these stores don't have a bulletin board, then ask if you can leave a small stack of business cards or brochures on their counter. Offer to put their cards or brochures at your barn in exchange. A nice clear plastic holder costs about $10 at an office supply store and will keep your brochures or business cards neat and out of the way. The holders also make you look more professional.

The Advertising Budget

Once you have a good idea of who your customer is and what he is actually buying, it is time to put together an advertising strategy.

Setting an advertising budget is the first step. This needs to be a realistic amount. The general rule of thumb is to set a budget that is 3% - 5% of anticipated gross. However, if you are operating at only a 3% profit margin, it is a little difficult to allocate that large a chunk to advertising. But, no matter how small your budget is, there are many ways to advertise. All that is required is a little time and creativity.

Frequency

Successful advertising must be seen or heard before a customer will respond. The closer the ad is seen or heard in relation to the time the customer makes the decision to buy, the more likely a customer is to react to it. The reason is simple a person is more likely to turn to you if they remember your name, if you and your business or product are familiar to them. Repetition breeds familiarity, familiarity breed trust, trust breeds sales. There have been countless studies on the number of times a person must see your name or message before they can remember it.

The average person must see or hear your message approximately twenty times before he will remember you and respond.

When I first started in this business, studies indicated that a message had to be seen or heard a minimum of seven times. Television, radio, cell phones, the internet, mail, e-mail, bulletin boards, magazines, news papers, newsletters have increased the need for frequency, because the number of messages the average American is bombarded with on a daily basis is massive. So now, instead of seven times, the average person must see or hear your message approximately twenty times before he will remember you and respond. If you spend you entire advertising on a single ad, you are not likely to get results. **It is much wiser to not place an ad _unless_ you can commit to running it a minimum of six times.**

Rates

Advertising rates can sometimes be confusing. Rates are generally determined by the number of people who read, listen to, or watch a given medium. In print media the number includes the actual *circulation* (how many actual issues are sold) and the number of estimated readers. Typically one person will buy a publication, take it home where other members of their household will read it, or they share the issue with friends. Radio rates are based on the number of people who are listening and will vary depending on the time of the day with morning and afternoon drive times usually having the largest listening audience. Television rates are determined by how many viewers are watching at a given time, generally associated with the popularity of a particular show. Typically, television stations have the largest viewing audiences during what is known as prime time, which varies according to the time zone – 8pm-11pm Eastern, 7pm-10pm Central, etc.

These numbers are usually determined by independent auditors who use sophisticated methods to find out the number of readers, listeners and viewers each individual publication, radio and television station has. They also help compile a profile of the audiences, including age, levels of education, household incomes, their principle hobbies or interests and how much they spend on them each year etc. Horse publication may even include the number and breed of horses owned, riding styles of their readers and the number of shows they attend each year.

All media have rate cards that list how much they charge for an ad. These cards or sheets of paper list the size or time options available to advertisers. Print media will have the sizes of print ads available. These sizes are either determined by modular units or column inches.

<u>Modular units are pre-set divisions </u>of the page such as a full page, half page, quarter page, 1/6 or 1/8 page etc. that are generally used by magazines or by column inches such a newspapers or other publications that have pages set up in columns.

<u>Column inches </u>are the number of inches or portion of inches your ad will occupy in a single column. An ad that is one column wide and one inch high is a one-column inch ad. If your ad is wider than one column, the rate is determined by multiplying the number of columns by the height of the ad. Thus a 2 column by 2-inch ad will be four column inches.

Radio and television advertisements are priced in time blocks, typically 60, 30, 15 and 10 seconds.

The price for each unit of advertising is determined by how large the number of readers, listeners and viewers a medium has. For print the audience size may be based on a per day audience as with daily newspapers, or a per-month, bi-month, quarter, semi-annual or annual basis depending on how often the publication comes out. For radio and television audiences are measured for blocks of time during a given day.

Advertising rates are not determined by the number of people in your target audience who may be reading, listening or watching. That is why you need to know who your audience is, compare it to the medium's demographics and determine approximately how many of your actual market you will reach with a given medium, then calculate your cost per thousand to see how much any medium is actually costing you to reach each of your potential customers.

The prices printed on rate cards are usually the cost per ad, with discounts given for more than one ad. The more often you run an ad the less EACH ad will cost. Regardless of how many times you run an ad the prices listed are generally for EACH AD, not the entire contract. Ads that are listed 6X $325, means that each ad is costing your $325 and the entire contract is $1950.

Typically, no matter how many times you contract to run an ad, you will pay for them on a monthly basis, and not be expected to pay the entire contract at once. However, you can usually save 10% or more of the total contract if you pay it all at the beginning, when you place your first ad. While this can be a sizable savings, I recommend that you not pay in advance for contracts with any medium until you see for yourself if it is going to work for you. A full payment in advance discount may not be such a bargain if you are paying for a medium that is not reaching your audience.

All ad prices are negotiable. This is a secret that most media don't want you to know. If a medium is trying to win your business, make them work for it by giving you a better price. You already know that you can save money by paying the entire contract in advance. You can also save by paying for a single ad at the time of placement, by providing camera-ready print ads, or pre-produced radio or television spots. If you save the medium the trouble and expense of producing your ads, you have every right to expect a discount of 15% to 25%. If you are trying a new medium, ask if they will sell you 3 ads at the 6-time rate or if they will sell you a ½ page ad for the 1/3 page price. If they won't agree to a lower price, see if they will ad color. You may not always get any of these discounts, but it doesn't hurt to ask.

Interestingly enough, when I was writing this portion, I mentioned it to a friend of mine who sells ads for one on the national horse publications. She said that while some publications might negotiate, they don't. "Really?" I asked. "You mean to tell me, if I was a new client and I asked for 3 ads at the 6 time rate, or if I asked for a ½ page at the 1/3 page rate, you wouldn't give it to me?" She paused a moment then said, "Well....possibly." The important thing to remember, when negotiating with the media, is not to make outrageous demands. Like you, they are in business to make money. They do so by selling ad space or time. They can't give it away, but if they want your business, they can be very helpful. Especially if you make it easy for them to do so by always getting your ad materials ahead of deadline and other things you will learn more about shortly.

Copy Writing

Copy in an ad is simply the words or text you use. Good copy writing is a craft that takes years to perfect. But great copy writing is an art form. Great copywriters, like great artists are born, not made and what they can do with words is astounding. If you aren't one of those lucky few that are born to write ad copy, there are some tips that will at least help you compose an effective ad.

First and most important is to remember what it is your customer is actually buying and craft your "BENEFIT message" so that it is selling exactly what the customer is buying. The benefit message in advertising tells the customer what is in it for them. An outstanding ad doesn't require much else beyond this message as long as the message is on target with your customers. A small ad with "Win More Ribbons" and your phone number can stimulate phone calls better than a larger ad that has lots of artwork and copy that overpowers or fails to include your benefit message.

In classified ads you will stand out far more, if you go against the custom of listing all the features of your business and simply put your benefit message and contact information.

I have a client with a boarding facility that had run a typical classified ad for two weeks with no real results. She called me and asked me to review her ad. I ended up doing a combination of benefit message and traditional feature listing. The end result was:

An effective ad only requires your strongest benefit message, and your phone number.

> *Want the very best care for your horse? Full turnout, box stalls, heated lounge, indoor arena, small herd size, personalized care and more! Call today. 555-555-5555*
> **xyz@fantasyfarms.net**

When she faxed the ad into the newspaper office, the person who read it called to tell her that the ad was so compelling she just had to call to find out more, and she didn't even own a horse. The day the ad ran her phone rang off the wall and by the end of the week her four empty stalls were full. The reason it worked was that we keyed in to a certain type of horse owner, one who wants the very best care for their horse. We promised to give it to them and then gave them a few facts to support out claim. The "best horse care" would require box stalls, full turnout, small herd and personalized care. The heated lounge and indoor arena were luxuries aimed at pampering the customer, not the horse, but they were chosen because we wanted to send the subtle message that if we are taking this good care of you, imagine how well we take care of your horse. Of course, all the ad did was get the customers to the facility. In the end if the client hadn't had a nice facility that looked like they were providing quality care for the horses, no one would have leased a stall.

So keep your focus on what it is the customer is really buying and don't clutter your ad up with a lot of information that isn't absolutely necessary.

When it comes to writing ad copy, less is best. In this age of ever increasing demands on our time, Attention Deficit Disorder is epidemic. People just don't have the time to read a lot of information. Give them the high points, the real emotional benefits of your goods or services and contact information. This is generally enough to get potential customers interested enough to contact you. Once they do, you can fill them in on more of the particulars as long as those particulars really underscore the emotional benefit you offer.

Design

Designing an ad can be tricky. It is a very involved process and quite often a matter of trial and error. Learning graphic design is not something you can do overnight. And if you don't plan on working in production or ad sales at a horse publication, you generally won't need to know more than a few basics to keep you out of trouble.

The actual design of an ad is called the layout. It shows where the copy or text, any art work, logo and contact information go. Like copy writing, good layout takes years to learn. I recommend that at the very least you check out a few books on graphic design from your local library, or purchase one of the books listed in the resource section at the back of this book.

I know that many computer word processing programs now have graphic art components, and that there are graphic design programs that do the same. Generally these programs are comprised of templates put together by supposedly professional graphic artists with the idea that, just by dropping your text (copy) into the predetermined positions, you will have a nice, professional looking ad. This sounds nice in theory, but the reality is that these fill in the blank ads still require some skill to use effectively.

Make sure customers know the benefit, that the benefit is strong, well-worded and neat.

First of all these ads tend to make your name or your company name the focus instead of keeping the focus on the benefit you offer your customers. In the ads I have seen where the selling point is more dominating in both size and position, the company name or the phone number tend to be the same size as the selling point. Don't ever do this. Unless you have a budget the size of Coca Cola's, no one really knows or cares who you are more than they care about what you offer them. As I have indicated many times before, the customer is extremely self-absorbed. He only wants to know how reading the ad and contacting you is going to benefit him. Make sure customers know the benefit, that the benefit is strong, well-worded and neat.

This may seem like the most obvious thing in the entire history of mankind, but always put your phone number in every ad and in every other marketing piece you ever put together. If customers are stimulated to respond, they have to have some way to do so. So make sure your ad includes your phone number, that the number is easy to find and to read, and that the number is correct. You would be amazed at how easy it is to get your own phone number wrong. To help prevent this, proof read it several times, ask other's to proof it and before you send it in, pick up the phone and actually dial the number to make certain it is correct. You would not believe how many people I know got no results from their ads because the phone number was wrong or left out.

If you have a web site, include its URL as well as your phone number. However before you send customers to your web site, make sure it is designed to sell your business, not simply give them boring information.

Unless customers will come to your business, or unless you have a very prestigious address, there is no need to include your address in an ad. If customers do come to your place of business and the address is not in a desirable area, don't include it in your marketing materials. Instead let customers call you to find out where you are located so that you have the opportunity to "sell" them on you before they are faced with an address they may find is farther out than they planned. Then, if the distance issue is brought, up you will have an opportunity to make the customer understand that what you offer is worth the drive. I drove my daughter 56 miles round trip four times a week for riding lessons even though there were closer barns. I did so because the trainer was well worth any inconvenience.

Ads in Reverse

As mentioned earlier, black is a powerful color. This is particularly true in standard black and white advertising. Most ads tend to have white backgrounds and to rely on artwork, a great layout or copy to get their ad noticed. Therefore if you want to stand out on a page, reverse the ad, make the background black and the type white. If all the other ads on the page have white backgrounds, this reversed ad will really get noticed. But, be careful with this design. Some fonts don't show up well in white against a black background and may become more difficult to read. Also, reversed ads in newspapers and magazines printed on news print paper can come out smeared or muddy looking and end up getting attention for all the wrong reasons. To avoid this, look through several issues of the publication you are considering advertising in and see how their reversed ads look. If they look good, chances are that yours will too. Keep in mind that if there are a number of reversed ads, you might want to change your mind about reversing yours. If there are too many reversed ads on a page the attention getting effect can be lost right along with your ad. The idea is to stand out, not blend in.

Color and Ads

Advertising is all about getting attention. In a print ad you are competing against all the other ads, plus the articles for the reader's attention. Color can increase the attention getting power of any ad, but you have to be careful in how you use it. If you are running an ad in a magazine that has a lot of color ads and photos, your color ad can get lost on the page. In such cases an ad that is black and white will generally stand out more. However publications generally put

Advertising is all about getting attention. In a print ad you are competing against all the other ads, plus the articles for the reader's attention.

all their full-color ads and photos on the same pages to keep printing costs down so it is difficult to get them guarantee that they will place your black and white ad in among a lot of full color ads. The best thing to do is to create an ad that is black and white and adding one more color for pop. In newspaper print ads, this black and white and one color layout can also work exceptionally well if it is an option.

Imitating Other Ads

While imitation may be the sincerest form of flattery, it can be deadly in advertising where individuality is critical. No matter how good someone else's ad is, if you make your ad look just like or similar to their ad, no one will notice you. In fact, what can happen is that readers will think that you are another ad for your competition. If you feel you must copy someone else's ad style, don't place it in the same publications. However, there is nothing wrong with taking a winning concept and making it uniquely yours.

In advertising, as in all marketing, the rule is "*Thou shalt steal and maketh it thine own.*" Find ads that really get your attention even if they are advertising a non-horse related goods or services. Figure out the elements that make the ad work- layout, artwork style, color use, or copy then adapt those elements to make an ad that is uniquely yours.

If you don't feel that you are capable of designing an effective ad, hire someone who is. If you can't afford an experienced graphic artist, then check with your local colleges or graphic art schools to see if they can recommend a student. A word of caution here, I have been in this business for a long time, and even I have trouble finding really good graphic artists. Make sure you ask to see samples of their work. Ask about charges and what they include. Don't allow a graphic artist to write or edit your ad copy or to convince you that the design is more important than the message.

Ad Size

Contrary to what ad sales reps may tell you, in advertising, size is not the key to effectiveness. Full-page ads are not necessarily better than smaller ads, and in some cases they can be less effective, especially if there are several full-page ads clustered together with no editorial pages in between. In such cases half or quarter page ads arranged on pages with a feature article or other editorial copy can be much more effective. So, if you don't have a large budget, and can't afford a page-dominating ad, one that takes up a sizable portion of the page, don't despair. A small ad can capture a lot of attention if you use a few tricks of the trade. First use fewer words and make the type very small. While large type may be easier to read, if the type is very small and surrounded by lots of blank space, it may stimulate the reader to look very closely just out of curiosity. The key in this kind of ad is to make sure that your benefit message is so strong or that you stimulate curiosity to the point that the reader just has to call to find out more.

Ultimately ad size is determined by your budget, the size of the overall page, the number of ads on a typical page, the amount of editorial copy included on the page, and how effective your ad is at calling attention to itself.

Camera-Ready

Most print media - newspapers, magazines, show programs etc. offer the advertiser two options:
1.) You can furnish them with camera-ready ads - the entire ad laid out to the correct size measurements, or
2.) They will put together an ad for you.

Unless you can afford to have an ad done for you by professionals, it is usually wiser to choose the second option. However, if you do so, you need to be sure to tell the person putting the ad together what your greatest benefits are to your customers. You will need to provide them with a good quality copy of your logo. You will also need to request at least one proof of the ad so that you can check to make sure that it doesn't look or read just like every other ad in the publication.

In addition to checking for uniqueness, check your phone number and address to make sure they are correct. Then check the rest of the ad for accuracy. Before your return the ad to the publication, have at least two other people review it for accuracy and readability. If you have to explain anything, either re-write it or take it out of the ad. No matter how good or important you may think a point in your ad is, if it has to be explained in order for it to have meaning for the reader, it needs to be removed. All copy in an ad must stand-alone because you can't possibly be there to interpret it for every reader.

Ad Agencies

Ad agencies can be a tremendous asset, particularly if the agency is familiar with selling to your market. Agencies usually make their money by getting a percentage of the cost of your ad (15% -20%) from the publication or radio or television station and from producing the printed or electronic ad. Because most agencies work on ad percentages, there is a push for expensive publications and electronic media. Naturally ad agencies want clients with budgets than can support more expensive ad media. Small businesses often have trouble finding an agency willing to work with them; however there are some around that are willing and able to do a good job. Most often though, it is a good idea for a small business owner to learn as much about advertising as you can if for no other reason than it will help you choose and get more from an agency.

Advertising Guidelines:

Ads are not meant to sell your services or products; Ads are meant to excite customers to call or come by your barn or business so that YOU can sell your service or products.

If your phone is ringing, the ad is working. If you aren't getting new business from those who are calling then you need to work on either 1.) The way you or your receptionist answers the phone, 2.) Your sales pitch - what you are telling the customer to sell them on you.

While some ads get immediate response most need to run at least 6 times before customers begin to pay attention to you.

❖ Test your ads in low cost publications before you move up to expensive ones.

❖ If you run a business card ad, make certain that your business card is actually an ad.

❖ If an ad doesn't work it may be the ad not the publication. Try a different ad before giving up on the publication.

❖ If an ad doesn't work it may be that the publication is not reaching your audience. Try the ad in a different better-targeted publication.

You will find ad samples and worksheets in the Appendix on pages xxxiii-xxxvi

<u>Chapter Eight</u>
Advertising Options

There are several options for your marketing communications that are used to get potential customers to pay attention to you and to remember you when they are ready to buy the goods or services you sell. You are probably more aware of these options than you realize. Signs, tack stall curtains, caps, t-shirts, jackets and other items with your business name printed on them, business cards, brochures, billboards, advertisements, web sites are all options that you should be familiar with. The secret to choosing which ones to use and having them work for you is to go for those options that reach the maximum number of your target market audience for the best price.

Keep in mind that your benefit message is just as important as where you place your ads. It doesn't matter how many potential customers see your ads, if you don't give them a real reason to respond and an easy way to do so.

Logos

Professional looking logos are an important part of your marketing. This is one area where professional help is highly recommended. Just having a computer program that can make up logos is not enough, unless you understand graphic design. It isn't simply a matter of choosing what you like. As with all marketing materials every aspect must be considered from the customer's prospective and its impact on them. Professionals should fully understand this and guide you to choosing the best font, colors, graphics, and design. The cost for a professional to design your logo can run from $150 - $3,000 depending on where you live and how detailed or intricate your logo is. If you are on a very tight budget, you may want to contact graphic design schools in your area and have them recommend a student to work with you. Before you turn the project over to a student or professional, ask to see samples of their work and get a written detailed estimate that lists all charges and exactly what they cover before work begins.

Once the logo is completed to your satisfaction, try to get a digital copy on computer disk and at least five hard copies of different sizes that you can have duplicated on a professional quality copier that will give you clean perfect images to use in advertisements etc.

If you feel that professional or student designers are beyond your budget, and you want to tackle designing your logo yourself, here are some general rules that will help you.

Logo design - Your logo is your professional "signature." It should be so unique that customers know it's you without reading the words, and should reinforce your chief benefit. Once you have a logo, use it in exactly the same form every time you put together an ad, business cards, letterhead, tack stall curtains, tack boxes, signs etc.

Logo Guidelines:

❖ Horizontal logos are easier to read than vertical ones.

❖ Use graphics that reinforce your benefit. Avoid meaningless geometric shapes and lines. (The Nike Swoosh works for them because the company has invested hundreds of millions of dollars in advertising specifically to generate recognition of the logo. As most horse businesses don't have that kind of ad budget, avoid geometric shapes.)

❖ Fight the temptation to use initials or acronyms as the name for your business. People remember words that create a mental image better than they do initials.

Warning: *Readability is more important than design.*
When using thin and/or decorative type or thick type, make certain they are as easy to read when they are business card and ad size as they are when sized for billboards.

You will find logo samples on pages xxx - xxxii of the Appendix.

Signs

Signs generally have to be read from the road while driving, therefore, it must be easy to read while on the move. When creating signs for your business, always test the layout for readability **before** you create the actual sign. To do so, ask your sign shop to print out a paper copy that is the same size and color as the final sign will be. If they don't offer this service, and you have a computer, print out the sign layout, or put your design on disk, take it to a local copy shop and have them print it out in full color in the same size as your final sign will be. This is called a "mock-up." Attach the paper mock-up to a wooden or cardboard backing and place it where the final sign will go. Drive by and see how well the sign stands out from the background and how easy it is to read while driving past. Does the sign seem to jump out from its surroundings? Can you read the name and phone number? You did put your phone number on it, right?

Ask friends to drive by to see how readable this mock sign is. When you ask friends to drive by, don't tell them to look for your sign. Just ask them to drive by to see if they notice anything different. Then call them and ask if they actually noticed anything. If they say no, change the sign design. If they say yes but then say they hate it, don't change the sign unless the majority of people who notice it tell you the same thing.

Producing this mock up of your sign may cost a bit, but in the long run it can save you a costly mistake. Paper printouts are a whole lot cheaper than paying for a sign, only to discover that no one can read it.

Prize Lists

School yearbooks or newsletters can be very reasonably priced advertising options, and if they allow it, so is your church bulletin or newsletter. Prize lists at local horse shows are a really great place for veterinarians, farriers, haulers, insurers, breeders, boarding facilities and trainers to advertise. If you have an EAP business prize lists are also a great place to advertise, particularly if you are specializing in treating eating disorders, child, adolescent or family counseling or behavioral disorders.

DON'T FORGET TO PUT YOUR AD IN ANY PRIZE LIST AND SHOW PROGRAM THAT YOU PRODUCE FOR YOUR OWN SHOWS. I am continually amazed at businesses that miss this prime advertising opportunity. In fact, make sure your ad is in more than one location in both your prize list and program. The best way to do this is to place a full page ad on the back of the front cover, then put a smaller ½ to ¼ page ad that sells another aspect of your business in one or two other locations inside the publication. Your competition may think you are conceited and a self-promoter, but who cares what they think. You will probably end up with their customers, which is why you are doing this in the first place.

NAHA Placemats

One of the best horse business advertising pieces I have seen is a paper placemat put together by the North American Horseman's Association, NAHA. This placemat has horse facts, photos and games in full color on both sides of the mat. There is also a space on the mat that says: *For more information about horses contact:* with room for you to put your name and contact information. The NAHA put the mat together specifically so that horse business owners would have an affordable and unique advertising outlet. The idea is that you purchase the mats and a stamp with your name and contact information. Once you have put all of your contact information on the mats, you take them to a local family restaurant or diner and ask if they would be willing to use the mats you supply for the children that come in with their parents. It is without a doubt one of the most cost effective, efficient advertising medium available. Because the NAHA prints these mats in such large quantity, you cost is about $.08 each plus minimal shipping charges.

Tack Stall curtains and the sides of trucks, and trailers are also great advertising tools if you treat them as such. While barn names are generally easy to find, how much more useful would these spots be if they included a phone number and/or web site?

I hope that at this point you are beginning to see that with a little imagination you can certainly find effective and affordable places to advertise your business.

It is important to remember that if you are aiming at more than one audience what is important to one group may not be what is most important to another. Again this is why you focus on one market segment at a time.

For example: When you are operating a boarding barn and lesson program, the people buying lessons are not always the same people that are buying horse board. Each group has a different need and will therefore require a different benefit. Does this mean you can't promote riding lesson and board in the same ads, flyers, or brochures? Does a person looking for a great place to board their horse care that you teach kids working towards national championships? Unless they are one of those kids, no, they don't. Does a person who doesn't own a horse and wants to learn to ride care that you offer the greatest boarding program in a three state area? Not particularly. And if you try to go after both market segments in the same promotional piece you will not be nearly as effective as you will with two separate pieces each aimed at a specific market segment. Of course it does not hurt to mention somewhere in each piece that you offer the other service. You just have to be very careful to assure that the we-also-offer service does not detract from the power of the benefit of the main service.

Brochures

Brochures quite often suffer the same fate as ads when it comes to computerized graphics and word-processing programs. The too much emphasis is placed on the company name and logo, and not enough on the benefits you offer the customer. The templates all have the business name and contact information on the front panel. The idea behind this placement choice is that if a person picks up the brochure, and doesn't read anything else but the front panel, they will at least have read your name so it isn't a total waste. Let me be the first to tell you that if a person picks up your brochure and doesn't open it, it **is** a total waste. It means that your benefit message either wasn't the right message for your audience, or it wasn't strong enough to generate enough curiosity to get the reader to actually open the brochure to learn more. If the reader doesn't care enough to do that, then remembering your name won't matter one wit. So don't put your name and contact information on the front of your brochures. Instead make the message strong enough so that the reader will open the brochure and learn so much meaningful and exciting information that when they finally get to your name and phone number they are ready to dial it.

The only exception to having your name on the cover is if you are as famous in the horse industry as someone like John Lyons or Monty Roberts. But then their names are not just the names of people, they are brands like Coke® and Nike®. Brands are names that are so strongly connected with a product or service that all you have to do is hear them or read them and you know immediately what they sell and its value. These folks have spent millions of dollars over a number of years developing that kind of brand recognition. As wonderful as you might be, unless you also have the same kind of brand recognition or the money to spend building it, leave your name off the cover of your brochures.

The other thing horse people are always putting on the cover of brochures is a drawing or photo of a horse. It makes sense; after all you are a HORSE business. Yes, well so are all of your competitors who also have photos or drawings of horses. If you want to stand out, wouldn't it be wiser to put pictures that reinforce your benefit, such as pictures of happy kids with lots of ribbons? If there happens to be a horse somewhere in the photo it shouldn't be more prominent than the students and their ton of ribbons. Of course if you are marketing to people that don't think winning is important then, by all means, avoid images of ribbons.

When you use images of people make certain that they are pictures of your target market audience. If you teach children, don't use images of adults and vice versa. If you specialize in shoeing hunter/jumpers don't use images of Arabians. If you teach barrel racing don't use images of reining.

EAP – almost every EAP business I have seen uses photos or drawings of horses. When I ask why they wanted to use a horse, they look at me as if I am insane and reply, "The horse is what makes

When you use images of people make certain that they are pictures of your target market audience. If you teach children, don't use images of adults and vice versa.

us different from all the other treatment programs out there." Wrong. What makes EAP different and more valuable to consumers than other forms of therapy is that EAP gets better results in a shorter period of time. That's the real benefit; the horse is just a tool. EAP businesses that treat young women with eating disorders need to have images of young girls who look happy and healthy – the result of effective EAP of course. If you are determined to use the image of a horse, at the very least make certain that the horse is interacting with a person who resembles your target market audience. DO NOT EVER USE AN IMAGE OF A PERSON ON A HORSE'S BACK in any of your EAP marketing materials. People already have a hard enough time with the concept that EAP is not riding lessons, don't confuse them more by reinforcing this incorrect assumption or it will really reduce the effectiveness of your materials.

Brochure Copy Writing

Writing copy for a brochure is similar to writing ad copy; the brochure just has more room. But don't let the space tempt you into telling more than you need to. The focus of everything in your brochure has to reinforce the benefit.

The outer page of a good brochure should include your strongest benefit message on the front panel. In the middle of the outer page, is where you place your mailing address and a space to put a customer's mailing address. The last panel is where you may want to put a short bio for you and key members of your staff.

Inside the reader should find a few sentences to support your benefit message, any statistics that support what you are saying, the five most important things you offer customers, testimonials from satisfied customers, a call to action – call now, call today, come see for yourself before it's too late, etc. and your contact information.

Tip: To help you fight the urge to over explain and write too much, try creating a single panel brochure – one that is 3 3/2 inches wide by 8 ½ inches high or the size of 1/3 of a normal page. Include all the elements listed above on this single panel. When you finish, drop the information into a regular 3 panel brochure format, and add space between the lines, and photos or facts that add impact to your original single panel brochure.

> **You can find a blank forms for creating your brochure in the Appendix on pages xx-xxv, and sample brochures on pages xxvi- xxix.**

Flyers

Flyers are a relatively cost effective way of advertising your business. Flyers work particularly well for special promotions such as a tack sale, clinic, or other occasional event. Most flyers are posted on bulletin boards. Again the key to their effectiveness is how noticeable the flyer is among the numerous other flyers on the same board. Spend sometime studying the competing flyers to determine how you can do yours differently. Keep the copy or text to a minimum and make sure the arrangement (layout) is neat and tidy but still interesting enough to capture attention. Use images that add strength to your benefit message and follow all the other principles of color, copy writing, layout and design in creating a winning flyer. Test the flyer by posting it on your own bulletin board or a friend's. Then quietly stand back and see if anyone notices it and if they react to it. If it doesn't work in this test, chances are that it won't work in a real promotional setting. To insure that your test is accurate, don't ask people what they think, just stand back and watch how they react. When you ask direct questions about marketing materials people tend to tell you what they think you want to hear, or what they think will make them appear smart. The best test is to see for yourself how they react.

A sample Flyer can be found on page xlv of the Appendix.

Business Cards

Business cards are the most common form of advertisement for small businesses. They can be incredibly useful in building name recognition. As valuable as business cards are, it is surprising to see how many horse professionals don't have them. This is particularly true of trainers and riding instructors. Most trainers will go through the trouble and expense of having professionally made tack curtains, and custom embroidered chairs, potted plants and such for their show stabling areas and yet not bother to have a $5 plastic business card holder, filled with striking business cards for any curious rider or parent to pick up and put in their pocket. I really have to wonder how much business they are missing out on by not doing this simple thing.

When most people think of designing a business card they think in terms of providing potential customers with their contact information - name, address, phone number, fax number, e-mail address and web site. While this is all well and good, for a business card to be the most effective requires a slight adjustment in thinking. A truly effective business card is not merely contact information it is a small advertisement. Everything about your card should reflect this fact. The quality of paper you use, the color of the paper and ink, the message on the card, the typeface or font used, and of course your logo should all be aimed at your specific audience and make you identifiable to them.

Think in terms of a good two-sided billboard in miniature and you have the right idea of what your business card should be. Most

A truly effective business card is not merely contact information it is a small advertisement. Everything about your card should reflect this fact.

folks make the mistake of leaving the back of their business cards blank. They don't seem to notice that when presented with a new card, the majority of people will turn the card over and look on the back. They are searching for more information and it is a critical error not to give it to them. It is also a lost opportunity to deliver your sales message – your benefits, and remind the customer who you are. Some will argue that printing both sides of the card almost doubles the cost. My argument is that the effectiveness gained, and the business generated by printing both sides is well worth the investment.

So let's talk about designing your card. Let's start with what is considered the back of the card first. If you have been reading this book from the beginning, you will know where to begin- with the benefits you offer your customer. This benefit tells the customer in a few short words what's in it for them, what they will gain by using your services or goods. Three or four of these benefits are important to selling your services and reminding the potential customer of what your business is about. List these benefits on the back of your card and you have transformed your business card into a sales tool. Be careful not to overload the card with too much information. You know it's too much if you have to reduce the font size to less than 6 points in order to get it to fit the available space. When it comes to benefits think in terms of few words and simple language. Don't tell the customer how they are going to get the benefit, just what the benefit is. If possible make your benefit part of a testimonial. For example: "Heavenly Valley Equine Assisted Psychotherapy helped me effectively reach clients in half the time." Sigmund Freud, psychologist. Or "Since I've been riding at XYZ stables, I've stayed in the ribbons." Sarah Joe, 3 time National Barrel Racing Champion.

Unless you have a professional design your cards, stay a way from light color inks or screens.

On the other side of your card, the front side, you should have your logo, the name of the person they should contact, the phone number, address and e-mail or web site address. I personally don't put my address on the card because customers don't come to my place of business and the only reason they ever have to mail me anything is when they pay an invoice. The invoice has the mailing address. I also don't include my fax number because I always give it to customers when they need it, and I don't want to overcrowd my card. You will have to make decisions on what goes and what stays, but remember that the customer has to know how to get in touch with you so that you can sell them on your services. The card doesn't sell you, you do.

When it comes to paper choices, textured papers work best. As with any message, the brain is more likely to store it, and recall it if you engage as many senses as possible. So go for something that your sense of feel responds to. When it comes to color, lighter papers are easier to read. Men prefer bolder colors while women prefer pastels and neutrals. If the majority of your potential customers are men, it would be wise to choose a bold colored, heavily textured paper. If the majority of your potential clients are women, then a smoother paper in a neutral or pastel tone will be the better choice.

All papers have a finish or sheen. The finish can be glossy, satin or flat. Glossy papers work well with full-color photo images. They also reflect more light and can be more difficult to read because of glare. Traditional wedding invitations are typically printed on papers with a satin or low to medium sheen. Men usually prefer glossy papers while women are more drawn to satin or kid finishes.

You can also add texture and interest to your business cards with several printing techniques – embossing, special cuts, foil stamping and thermographed inks are some of the choices. The first three choices tend to be very expensive and out of the price range of most horse businesses. Thermographed inks can also cost more than regular inks, but not tremendously so and can add a lot to your card. Thermograph printing requires the use of special inks that will "puff up" when heated. This results in the lettering and printed images sitting on top of the paper instead of lying flat as traditional printer inks. I have often gotten the effects of expensive embossing by using the more affordable thermographed inks.

The most important think to consider when choosing inks should always be readability first.

When it comes to ink colors look for those that offer the highest contrast to your paper color. Unless you have a professional design your cards, stay a way from light color inks or screens. The only consideration for ink colors is READABILITY. The easier it is to read, the better. When in doubt, there is nothing wrong with plain white paper and black ink. However, if you go this route make certain that your overall design stands out from your competition. The purpose of your business card is to identify you.

Business Card Guidelines:

❖ Keep it simple and brief.

❖ Only include information that really matters. Fax numbers, e-mail addresses can be given to people once they become customers. Unless customers come to your place of business, you don't have to include your address.

❖ Focus on your benefit message.

❖ Use colors and images that are meaningful to your customer.

❖ Printing information on the back of the card is more important than using more colors or a nicer paper.

❖ Using more than one color ink is more important than using an expensive paper.

Sample business cards can be found on page xlii of the Appendix.

Web sites

In this day and age, almost every person owns a computer. Each day thousands of these computer owners are logging on to the Internet. While I don't think that the Internet will ever live up to its publicity, it can be a valuable marketing tool.

If you strip away all of the hype and technical aspects of the World Wide Web, it is ultimately an electronic mail order catalogue, library and directory service. Just as mail order catalogues did not replace retail stores, the Internet is not going to, at least not anytime soon. Land's End has a mail order business that has been successful with old-fashioned printed catalogues and a web site. Despite this they have recently begun selling their products in Sears stores. Sears, itself a strictly mail-order business for decades, abandoned its mail order business in favor of retail stores years ago when the rising cost of printing and postage, and a drop in mail order revenues made it unprofitable. Sears recently got back into mail order when Internet shopping eliminated the need for expensive printed catalogues and the postage to end them to customers.

The Internet is all about speed. No one is going to spend the time looking through a lot of junk to find what he or she need.

For non-mail order businesses, the web is like an enormous phone book. Its very size is its biggest problem. If people type in "riding stables," they are going to get thousands of listings. They will have to go through a list that has no particular order beyond that determined by how many times a particular word or words appear on the site's home page. If you live in Atlanta, GA, and you are looking for a local barn you may have to go down a list that has dozens of barns in Europe and Japan before you get to even one within driving distance of your home. If that same person goes to one of the web yellow pages directory, they might be able to find you, if they know your business name and then all they will find is your street address and phone number, not your web site. Typically a potential customer is only going to visit your web site if she already knows your name and web site address. So, your web site's usefulness is greatly determined by how good a job you do in marketing your business and its web site.

It is a rare horse business that benefits greatly from a web site, and none that depend solely upon the web to market themselves.

Of all the horse related businesses that can benefit from having a web site, tack shops, organization and associations, residential treatment centers that use EAP, breeding and horse sales sites and colleges and schools with riding programs are at the top of the list.

To get the most out of any web site, there are a few things you need to understand. People go to web sites looking for information. You know all those features that were supposed to take a back seat to your benefits in your other marketing materials? Well, a web site is the perfect place to put them. But, your home page should be all about your benefit, and that benefit should be emphasized on every page. If your benefit is that you train winners – then every page on your site should have images that show winners. If your benefit is a huge selection of products at great prices, you should have the price generally charged by your competitors for each item along with what you charge and how much of a savings it represents.

Don't forget that providing all the information in the world won't do you a bit of good if potential customers can't find it and find it quickly. The Internet is all about speed. No one is going to spend the time looking through a lot of junk to find what he or she need. All those beautiful graphics and photos of your facility won't help a bit, if they take too long to download. The KISS principle applies to Web sites just like it does to all other marketing materials. If you want results - Keep It Simple Stupid.

If you are a college with a riding program, a potential student should be able to easily and quickly find the link to your equine or riding program's pages on your college home page. If they have to go through a process that makes sense to your Webmaster, chances are they won't find what they're looking for and move on to the next college with a riding program.

Always test your web site. The best way I have found to do this is to put together a small group of the primary target market. I ask them what items of information are most important to them when they are searching for information on businesses such as my clients. I ask them to rank the items by importance. Once I have that information, I find a few folks with limited Internet experience to come to my client's business. I set up several computers and have the test group go to the web site and find five to ten items. (I prefer using older people who have not grown up with computers because, if they can find their way around the site, visitors with more experience will certainly be able to.) I then stand back and watch the process. I use a stopwatch to time how long it takes them to find each item. If it takes longer than a few seconds, the site designer has to change the site to shorten the process.

If your web site designer or webmaster can provide it, a means of tracking user movement on your site can also help you identify problems and correct them.

Web site Guidelines:

❖ Always provide a means for visitors to give you their contact information. "For more information" is one of the best ways to get them to do this. These words should be on every page and have a link. Then when the viewer clicks on that link they should go to a page that has a fill-in-the-blank form for them to put in their name, e-mail address and any questions along with the your phone number so that they can call if they prefer.

- ❖ Always have your contact information on every page. If the visitor decides he wants to contact you, it has to be easy for him to find out how.

- ❖ Always give site visitors a reason to contact you, and ask them to do so.

- ❖ Answer inquiries generated by your site as quickly as possible. If someone is on the web looking for particular goods or services, you can bet yours isn't the only site she has gone to. The faster you respond, the more likely you are to end up with the customer.

- ❖ If the percentage of visitors who actually contact you is very small, change your site.

- ❖ Make sure that your Webmaster checks the site frequently to make sure everything is working as it should.

- ❖ Correct problems with the site immediately.

A sample web site can be found on page xliv of the Appendix.

Newsletters

When it comes to building a business, particularly a service business a newsletter can be a tremendous tool. Newsletters afford you the opportunity to tell your story, your way. This allows you to communicate your benefit message to your existing and potential clients better than most ad campaigns, at least is can if it reflects the benefits your barn or lesson program offers.

If your target market is predominantly kids, then it is important to make every story in your newsletter reflect the things that are meaningful to kids, and their parents. If you work mostly with adults, then tailor your articles for them. Articles on barn safety and various tips on things such as how to be a great pony mom or horse show dad would serve to show parents that you understand their position and that they are valuable to you, which helps increase their customer loyalty which in turn increases their support both financially and emotionally.

Posting used tack and horses for sale, your rider's latest show results, profiles of school horses, profiles of employees (especially new employees), new equipment, barn birthdays of horses and riders gives you an opportunity to let people know more about your barn, how exciting and fun your barn is and to demonstrate how much you appreciate your customers. Everyone, regardless of age or gender likes, to see his and his horse's name and photos in print. Posting wins will not only make your clients feel good, it sends a subtle message to potential clients – we produce winners, which may bring them to your doors.

A word of caution – don't focus only on your super stars. If you adopt the attitude that everyone in your barn is a star worth writing about, your newsletter and your business will reflect it, which will increase your business and income. A rider who has finally mastered something that was very difficult for her is worth bringing to the attention of your readers. It sends the message to your existing clients, and potential clients that you don't have to be the best to be worth writing about and that all of your riders are equally important to you.

Include articles on improvements made to your facility and any new services or special offers that you are offering. This is the one place that you can really blow your own horn and have it work for you. If you have improved the footing, added new paddocks, designed a new logo, purchased new tack stall curtains, or a new trailer put the story and a photo in your newsletter so that everyone. Quite often clients will stop coming because of something like poor footing and never tell you. If they read in your newsletter that you have replaced the footing, they might decide to come back. The potential for this kind of reaction is reason enough to include all improvements you make to your facility and equipment. Furthermore, improvements indicate growth, growth indicates success and almost everyone wants to do business with someone they perceive as successful.

You may be able to use samples of your newsletter to land an assignment to write and article or column for magazines and newspapers.

Keep the tone of your newsletter friendly and conversational. When you sit down to write, it may help if you think about talking on paper. Pretend you have a client you really like sitting across from you and you are going to tell them all the fun, new and interesting things going on in your barn or lesson program. Use photos of your riders, boarders and their horses. Ask your clients to take photos of things that they like about your barn and encourage the kids in your barn to create drawings of your barn and horses and use them as art work in your newsletter. Be sure to give the artists and photographers credit.

If writing is not your talent, you might consider contacting a local college with a journalism or mass communication program to see if there is an upper class student who would be willing to serve as editor of your publication. Students generally work for much smaller fees than experienced professionals and can generally do a good job for a reasonable cost.

Publishing software that is fairly easy to learn, and allows you to print out copies yourself are a good investment. If you want to save the cost and time of printing you can create your newsletter in a publishing program and then convert it to an Adobe PDF file using Adobe Acrobat 6. You can then send the newsletter via e-mail to everyone in your barn and post it on a web site if you have one. If you can't afford to purchase Adobe Acrobat 6, www.adobe.com offers a low cost means of converting your work to a PDF file. Graphic design students can help you create a template for your newsletter that will allow you or your student editor to simply drop in art work, photos and text.

A good length for most newsletters is 4 pages – 2 pages front and back. If you print them out on standard 8.5" X 11" paper, be sure to staple them together. It's neater and easier to read. Keep copies of your newsletters and put them into ring binders that you leave out in your office or lounge area so that visitors and new comers can read through them to see what a great barn you have. If you become really good at writing a newsletter, you can use samples to show magazine and newspaper editors your writing skills and perhaps land an assignment to write and article or column for them. This is a great way to increase your credibility.

The keys to successful billboard advertising are placement, message and design.

While the looks and content of your newsletter are important, to be most effective, newsletters must be distributed on a regular basis, each month, every other month, every quarter, semi-annually or annually. As long as your readers know when to expect the newsletter, they will learn to expect it and to look forward to it. If however, you produce the newsletter whenever the mood strikes; your audience pays less attention to it. I recommend that newsletters intended to build a business be published at least every quarter. For most people, publishing 4 newsletters a year is about all they can manage. If you have a passion for publishing, by all means plan to do 6 or 12 a year. Just make sure that you don't commit to doing them, then become so overwhelmed with the time and expense involved that you only publish sporadically. Plan a reasonable publishing schedule and stick to it.

Regardless of whether you print your newsletter on paper or distribute it electronically, you might be able to offset the cost of its production by soliciting sponsorship from area tack shops and feed stores with whom you do business. Offer to include their ad in your newsletter as part of the sponsorship. You may not get any takers, but it never hurts to ask.

> *You can find examples of horse business newsletters at www.HorseBusinessAssociation.com and http://www.vic.edu/ frameset.html?/academics/degrees/index.shtml&1 to view the Virginia Intermont College Equine Studies newsletter, The Hoof Beat.*

Billboards

Billboards are not the best advertising choice for everyone or every circumstance. They can be expensive to produce and, if they are not in a high traffic area, can get very poor results. That being said, for some, billboards are the best possible choice.

The keys to successful billboard advertising are placement, message and design. Message is of course the benefit. The problem is that people are reading your billboard while driving. They don't have much time. The general rule of billboard copy is to keep it down to 10 words or less with your phone number or web site counting as one word.

The most important aspect of billboard design is readability and noticeability. No one is going to read your ten words if they don't notice the billboard in the first place. So make sure your billboard will stand out from the background scenery and the other billboards. Placement is far more critical to the overall effectiveness of billboards than it is for any other form of advertising. For horse businesses, the single best placement for a billboard is along those highways and roads that lead to and from the major competitions that your target audience attends.

For example: I have a client with a quarter horse breeding operation. He is new, small and in an area with a number of other quarter horse breeders. He has a well-known stud and happens to be just off the interstate that is heavily traveled by people who compete at a number of very large, AQHA shows. For him, the best possible advertising was billboards along this interstate. We started with two billboards, one visible to all these competitive AQHA folks traveling north to the competition and one for those traveling south. It didn't take long for him to feel the positive impact of his billboard campaign.

Billboards Guidelines:

❖ Limit the words to 10 or less with your phone number or web site being one of the words.

❖ Keep the design easy to read but interesting enough to grab attention and stand out from the scenery and other billboards.

❖ Avoid background colors that blend in with surrounding buildings, trees, sky, etc.

❖ Place your billboards along routes that are heavily traveled by your target market.

You can find a billboard layout sheet on page xxxvii of the Appendix.

Radio & Television

If you have the budget to afford it, radio and television can be very good advertising options. As with all advertising, repetition is vital to effectiveness. Just as placement is important to a billboard campaign's success, timing is important to the effectiveness of radio and television campaigns. Radio and television stations determine their rates by how many people are listening or watching at a particular time of day. The more listeners or viewers during a time slot, the higher the fee for ads that are aired during that time slot. The lowest cost advertising schedule for radio or television is called ROS or run of station. This means that you pay for your ads to run whenever the station wants to run it during its entire broadcast day. If a station is on the air for 24 hours a day your ad or ads could run anytime during that 24 hours schedule. If a station is on the air from 5 a.m. until 11 p.m., your ad or ads could run anytime from 5 – 11.

This means that, while it costs less overall to run your ads ROS, the overall effectiveness will be reduced. Your actual cost per listener may be much higher than if you ran your ads during a high listening time.

Ultimately, how well you spend your ad budget, and how effective the ads you create are, are much more important than how much you spend on advertising.

Generally speaking, radio advertising will work best if you are a retail store, have a riding lesson or board program, or are promoting a special event. Radio works for these purposes because almost every town has a radio station that has a large number of female listeners who are either of riding age, or have children who may be interested in riding.

Typically, I recommend running radio ads during traffic reports. Almost every radio station has updates on how the traffic is flowing during peak drive times. This means that the number of listeners is very high, usually the highest of the broadcast day because everyone who is on their way to work or on their way home are listening to determine what route they may want to take, or what alternate routes they may need to use once they are in route. Radio stations usually require that advertisers running during the traffic reports agree to do so for a minimum number of weeks, which will give you the repetition that you need.

If there are talk radio stations in your town with programs that pull a large female audience, such as Dr. Laura, running your ads in and around this show may be the best choice for you.

My experience has been that radio sales representatives know their medium and audiences, and can be very helpful in creating your ad. However, you must know what it is you are selling, who you are selling it to, and the BENEFIT you want to emphasize.

In this day and age, 30 seconds ads are not only more affordable than 60-second ads, they are more effective when used to reach audiences who have ever shrinking attention spans. In addition to the 30 and 60-second ad option, many stations offer 10 second "billboards." Of course the shorter the ad, the more skill and talent are needed to make the message meaningful to your audience and effective at spurring them to contact you.

Because of the cost of television advertising the only television I recommend to businesses with small budgets is the banner that runs at the bottom of the local weather channel. Contact your local cable provider for cost and frequency information.

Best Options for a Small Budget

- The classified section of your local newspaper.

- Your local weekly television-listing guide.

- Your local entertainment guide.

- Local parent publications.

- The banner on the Weather channel through your local cable network.

- Local cable stations during horse programs that relate to your type of lessons or appeal to your audience - i.e. rodeo, bull wrestling, grand prix horse shows, equine vet shows.

- Local horse show or rodeo programs.

- Local college newspapers.

- County agent publications.

- Church bulletins and newsletters.

- School year books and newsletters.

- 4-H publications.

Your choices for advertising options should be determined by the results of your student or customer profile.

Chapter Nine

Public Relations

If you get 12 public relations professionals in a room and ask them what public relations is, chances are you will get 12 different answers. The best definition for our purposes is that public relations are any promotion of your business that is not paid advertising. This includes newsletters that you send to your existing or potential clients, coverage by the local press or news programs, appearances on talk shows, down to answering your phone and how you treat you customers on a regular basis.

Press Coverage

Most business people, including sadly some who are public relations consultants, tend to think that the way to get their name and message in the newspaper or on the radio or television is to bombard the media with press releases about everything. In reality the best way to get your name in the game is to do something newsworthy.

For example: If a horse show or rodeo is coming to town, and you have a student who has worked their way back from an injury in order to compete or if you have a student who is incredibly young or old to be in the competition, call the features editor of your local paper and the producer of your local radio and TV news programs and let them know. Ask if they would like to come out and in the case of television, tape some footage of this rider for their evening news or morning show. You should ask print media if they would be interested in coming to take photos or do a write up.

Another example: You have started a carriage service for weddings. You read in the paper that a local politician or his/her child is getting married. Contact the politician and offer your services free of charge, ask if they would mind if you contacted the media to let them know the dates and times so that they can be on hand to tape the affair. Generally speaking politicians never turn down an opportunity for press coverage, unlike celebrities who may want privacy. In the unlikely event that the politician says no, ask if they would mind if you hired a professional

photographer to take photos so you could send one or two of the best photos to the paper after the event.

General Rules for Getting Press Coverage

❖ Develop a press form so that every time you have a student place in the top three at a horse event you can send it into the paper along with a photograph. See *Sample Press Release* at the back of this book.

❖ If a reporter calls stop what you are doing and give him your full attention. Reporters work on deadlines. They can't afford to wait and, if they can't get you, they will find someone else.

❖ Answer reporter's questions in a forthcoming manner, in a respectful, pleasant tone. Do not disparage others and be careful about making negative comments. Do not lie or provide exaggerated claims. Just like you, reporters appreciate those who take the high road.

❖ Keep your expectations small. Quite often an hour of interviewing results in a single line or quote or less. Depending on how the story goes or how much space is available, or entirely at the editor's whim, anything can happen. Take it in stride and be pleasant and understanding in future dealings with them. Don't take it out on the reporter.

❖ Don't try to manage the press. If you want control, buy an ad. If you want publicity, you have to accept that you are at the reporter's mercy. **<u>Never</u>** ask to see a final copy of the article before it goes to press. Accept that the final article may not contain the "story" that you wanted. The reporter and his editor determine what angle to use, depending on his/her needs and the information the reporter gathers. Chances are the final article may not be entirely accurate. Take the mistakes in stride and don't complain to the reporter.

❖ If you are misquoted don't complain. Reporters really do try to get it right, but it is very difficult to take notes verbatim, particularly when the human brain doesn't always hear or interpret it the way you intended. Chances are that you will be misquoted. Unless it is truly a libelous or slanderous comment, don't worry about it. If you complain to the reporter, or worse, his editor, you will never again get favorable coverage from that publication again. And, if that reporter goes to another medium, which is highly likely, you won't get coverage from his new publication or TV or radio news program either.

Quite often an hour of interviewing results in a single line or quote or less in the final article.

- When you send out a press release or contact information to the medial, include several contact numbers where you can be reached during the day, night and weekend, mobile phone, pager or other numbers. Reporters need to be able to reach you at their convenience not yours.

- Understand that, typically, daily newspapers, radio and TV schedule articles one-day to three-months before publication. Magazines schedule articles anywhere from 2-3 months to one-year before publication date. How much advance time a particular medium requires depends on their editorial calendars, seasonal coverage and breaking news. If you are having an event on the same day the president's limo blows a tire, your article or TV coverage may be pulled and run on a later date or dropped completely.

- If you want copies of an article or tape of a story or interview, do not ask the reporter for them. Pick up a copy of the publication or call the media outlet to order a copy or tape.

- Research the media you are interested in being covered by. If you want to improve your chances of getting a story covered, you need to be familiar with the kinds of stories they run. Read a publication, listen to the radio or watch the particular TV show you are interested in. The better you understand the kind of stories they are interested in the better your chances of selling them on your story idea.

If you want to improve your chance of getting a story covere you need to be familiar with the kinds of stories the medium run

- Once your story appears, take the time to send the reporter a note thanking him for doing such a fine job on the story. DO NOT mention any errors or other problems you may have with the final product. Remember you want to make sure that the reporter's encounter with you is so positive that, the next time he needs any contact for a horse related story, you are the first one he calls.

- Plan at least 2 newsworthy events each year. For example: Host a clinic conducted by a perceived expert in the field who is from more than 100 miles out of your town.

- Don't contact editors or producers unless you have something special to sell them on.

- Don't contact a media person more than once every 3 months unless you have a once in a lifetime opportunity that will interest his readers, listeners or viewers.

- If you invite the media, serve them food.

- Give the media at least 2 weeks notice so they can arrange to have cameras and reporters assigned.

- Give the media a reminder the day before the event.

- Have a back up plan to tape or photograph the event in case

the media has a preemptive event at the last moment and can't make the event at your facility

Press Releases

Press releases are short articles that you send to the media to advise them of the basic facts of an event or accomplishment that involves you or some aspect of your business. A good press release has a really interesting first sentence that captures the reader's attention, followed by who, what, when, where, why and how. Not necessarily in that order.

It is a good idea to send out press releases when you open a new business or expand an existing one, as well as every time you or one of your students places in the top three in a competition. Newspapers love photos of kids doing something interesting so even if your student comes in 6th out of 16, a press release accompanied with a photo stands a good chance of getting in the publication. This kind of press release makes students feel important, which builds customer loyalty and attracts new customers.

Press releases can be sent to all media in your area including TV and radio newsrooms, newspapers, and magazines. These outlets get hundreds of these releases a day, so the better yours is, the more likely it is to be chosen.

Always type your press releases and include your contact information at the top right hand corner. Make certain that you include all phone numbers where you can be reached. If the press release is about an event that is coming up, such as a large horse show, make certain that you write FOR RELEASE ON OR BEFORE (THE DATE) in all caps, centered above the title. Format the press release so that it has one-inch margins and is double-spaced. Don't forget to check for spelling and grammatical errors. Don't rely on your computer's spell checker to do this for you. Print it out and proof read and get at least two other people to proof it after you.

Call and find out to whom you need to send your press release. In most cases it will be the lifestyle, sports or women's section editor at a publication or the assignment editor at a radio or TV news show. Verify the correct spelling of this person's name. Mail or e-mail the press release to the proper person.

The more professional the release looks, the more interesting it is, and the easier it is for a reporter to get in touch with you, the more likely he is to run your release. If he or his editor is intrigued by the information, a reporter might call you to do a feature article.

If the competition or event is large enough or important enough and the student wins or places in the top three in the event, it is a good idea to have this information together but instead of sending it in, call the features editor of your local paper and let them know just how important the win is and what a great human interest story it would be for their readers. If you do a good job of convincing them, they should ask to interview you and the students along with the family if it is a young child or if the family is well known.

A Sample Press Release is on page xliv of the Appendix.

Following is a press release I wrote to promote a training for Equine Assisted Psychotherapy. I didn't care if the media ran this release as is. I just wanted an unusual enough opening to grab attention and create interest. It worked. The local papers didn't run the release, instead they sent their own reporters out to cover the event. The end result was that we got a lengthy feature story complete with photos.

The Critical Parts of the Press Release

Contact: Lanier Cordell
225 262-6617 —— Contact Info for the Media

FOR IMMEDIATE RELEASE, PLEASE. ——————— Release Date

PSYCHO HORSES RUN AMUCK AT VIRGINIA INTERMONT COLLEGE
—— Attention Grabbing title

Crazed horses with teeth bared charging at everyone in their path; a misunderstood equine lounging on a sofa pouring out tales of a troubled ponyhood or relationship problems with an owner are the kinds of mental images the average person has when they first hear of Equine Assisted Psychotherapy.
—— Compelling opening sentence (a.k.a. the Hook)

"Ever since we announced plans to offer a certification workshop in Equine Assisted Psychotherapy this February, we have spent a lot of time dispelling these kinds of misconceptions," says Eddie Federswich, director of Intermont's Equine Studies Program. "The truth is that Equine Assisted Psychotherapy is not emotional therapy for horses, it is a new and growing form of therapy that uses horses as a tool for treating troubled humans."
—— What
—— Who

The workshop that prompted all this discussion is a three-day Equine Assisted Psychotherapy certification program sponsored by Virginia Intermont College. The workshop will be held at the VIC Riding Center in Bristol, VA February 14-16, presented by one of the creators of the inter-nationally recognized program, Lynn Thomas of Equine Assisted Growth and Learning Association.
—— What
—— Where & When

Horses communicate primarily with non-verbal cues – the position of their ears, their heads, the arrangement of their feet, and the movement of their tongues are all indicators of their mood. Add to this equation the fact that the average horse has no desire to communicate with you or to do what you want him to do. In many ways the behavior of horses is similar to the average human adolescent.

The theory behind Equine Assisted Psychotherapy is that if you can teach people to communicate with horses and gain their cooperation, these skills can be used to better communicate with other humans and to deal with a wide a variety of emotional and relationship problems.
—— How & Why

"Most horse owners already understand the benefits of mastering the skills involved in developing a bond with their horses," says Federwisch. "The Equine Assisted Growth and Learning Association has developed a program that adds these benefits to a specially developed therapy program which has demonstrated phenomenal success nationwide."

EAGALA began at a residential treatment facility for adolescents where the kids had the opportunity to work with horses. The change the relationship with the horses brought about in these yound people was the beginning of what has grown into the outstanding EAP program taught in Equine Assisted Psychotherapy seminars and workshops throughout the country.

"It's our goal to bring the use of horses in psychotherapy to a very professional level with set standards of practice and tools for evaluation," says Thomse, who holds a masters in social work, has extensive experience working with adolescents and families and is have developed a system based on the professional Equine Assisted Psychotthe director of EAGALA. The EAGALA systerm is based on therapeutic team, which consists of a qualified equine professional and a licensed therapist. The team develops and institutes treatment plans for each individual, family or group participating in the therapy session. Together the team helps clients learn to maneuver the horse through various obstacles and past different forms of temptation. According to a study done by Douglas Mann, L.M.F.T., Licensed Marriage and Family Therapist, adding a horse to the psychotherapy toolbox can be a tremendous aid that increases success rates while reducing rehabilitation time. To continue to move Equine Assisted Psychotherapy to a higher level of professionalism, the Equine Assisted Growth and Learning Association, (EAGALA) has developed a manual and certification program complete with tests to verify a standard of expertise. Their program is the basis for Virginia Intermont College's social work minor in Equine Assisted Growth and Learning, the first of its kind in the country.

"At Intermont, we are making every attempt to be on the cutting edge of developments in the horse industry," says Federwisch. "We consider the use of horses in therapy to be very cutting edge.

The Equine Assisted Psychotherapy certification workshop is open to all interested therapists, family and marriage counselors, psychiatrists, psychologists, guidance counselors, corrections officers and horse professionals. Continuing Education Credits may be available for up to 24 hours. Check with your state licensing board for approval. EAGALA is a continuing education provider for NAASAC, MFT, LCSW, and LPC in California, Florida and Texas. Applications have been submitted to NASWLA and LA Counseling Association for continuing education units. For further information on the 3-day workshop and how to sign up, contact the Intermont Riding center at (276) 669-8398. For more information on Equine Assisted Psychotherapy, please contact Lynn Thomas at (801) 754-5886.

# # # #

Local Interest- Mentioning the local school and their minor program will increase the local media's interest

Details and contact info for the workshop's market

Feature Articles

Feature articles are the lengthy articles in magazines and newspapers. The television equivalent is human-interest stories on your local news. Feature articles are generally accompanied by photographs and are much larger than most press releases. These articles tend to have a human-interest slant. Feature articles are a tremendous business builder. They are more effective than paid advertising because people know that you didn't pay for it, so anything good that is said about you must be true.

The best way to pursue a feature article is to read several issues of the publication you want to be in and get a feel for the kind of stories they like and if there is some aspect of your business that is similar. By similar I do not mean exactly the same. If a local publication runs a feature on a local riding lesson program, they are not going to run another story about a riding lesson program again for years, unless there is something so special and unique about your program that they feel their readers or viewers will really want to know about it.

There are several books available on how to get free press that can be valuable in your search for media coverage. Invest in one. Your other option is to contact a local college or university's journalism department and see if they can recommend a senior student to help you construct a press release or query letter. If you can afford it, a public relations professional can be a very wise investment. I recommend that if you hire someone in this capacity that you clarify what you are going to be charged and what the fees cover. There are no guarantees with news coverage, a great story that everyone at a particular medium was so hot for, can be dropped like a hot potato if something better comes along. You could end up paying a lot of money and end up with nothing to show for it. So be cautious of PR people who promise you that they will get you into national publications. Ask for some verification that they have the contacts to do what they are promising. Look at samples of their work. Ask for the names and contact information of several clients. Then contact these people and ask what the PR professional did for their money and if they are satisfied with the results.

A constant flood of uninteresting press releases and feature article requests will make editors and reporters turn a deaf ear to your pleas for press.

Be cautious about contacting the media too often. If an editor or reporter gets press releases and feature article requests from you constantly on uninteresting things, he will become deaf and blind to your pleas for press.

Don't ask for news coverage unless you are doing or have done something truly newsworthy.

Contributing Columns or Articles

If you happen to have a lot of talent, or knowledge in a particular aspect of the horse industry, and a talent for writing, then contributing a column or articles to local, regional and national magazines may be a great option for promoting your business.

Having your name or by line on a column or article that is read by your potential customers is without a doubt the best way to build a reputation, which in turn builds your business. It can also be a great way to earn a little extra money with your expertise. National magazines can pay very well. But unless you plan to make you're living as a writer, don't worry about how much a publication pays for your column or article. Even if you write for free, having your name appear as writer of an article sets you miles ahead of your competition.

If you are interested in pursuing writing columns and articles, it would be wise to read books on the subject or even take a journalism class or two. The rewards of being an "expert" in print or other media are well worth the investment of time and money.

I write marketing columns in three horse publications and am frequently contacted by writers working on articles about the horse industry, particularly articles about college and school riding programs. My association with the Intercollegiate Dressage Association and Virginia Intermont College's Equine Studies has put my name before a number of editors and writers. I am now considered a resource for articles on college equine programs and degrees as well as other aspects of the horse industry. This reputation makes it possible for me to get press for my clients, my organization and my business. It has evolved because the horse world is quite small; word gets around. Any time a reporter or writer or ad rep contacts me, I do whatever I can to help them. If I don't know something about what they are looking for, I have a list of experts in many areas of the horse industry. I gladly share their names and contact information. The reason is simple. If I don't have the information for one particular story, if I help the writer find someone who can, you can bet that the next time the writer needs someone with my information, she'll call me first.

Other Ways to Get Your Message Out

Find out if your library or Chamber of Commerce has a speakers list for "experts" in your town. Have yourself added to the list for your area of horse expertise. Take the time to prepare talks on different topics. You may hate the idea of giving speeches but, with practice and preparation, the nervousness and awkwardness goes away. And the business you could build through public speaking is tremendous.

Community organizations such as the Kiwanis Club are constantly looking for speakers for their meetings. Call and get yourself on the schedule to talk about what is happening in the local horse community and what it means to them. While females are more likely to be interested in horses and horse matters, than most men, men are also fathers, husbands and boyfriends who may have a daughter, wife, sister or girlfriend who is horse crazy.

Contact your local college to see if they offer leisure courses and if you can teach one on an area that will interest horse owners; i.e. horse care for the first time horse owner or whatever you think will appeal to the largest audience of horse people. Ask your customers for topics they would be interested in learning more about.

Communicating with Your Customers

Most businesses that fail do so because they don't communicate well with their customers. If you want to build a business, you have to build client loyalty and the only way to develop client loyalty is to listen to what your customer wants or doesn't want and to tell them what you want or don't want in return. It sounds simple, but for some reason people in the horse business are better at communicating with horses than they are at communicating with people.

To better communicate with your customer:

❖ Put your barn policies, your services and the charges for them in writing and make sure every new customer who enters your place of business gets a copy.

> **For example:** If you have a show barn, you should have a special price sheet that includes all services provided for students who show and the cost of each. Designate which services are mandatory and which are optional. If you require that all students showing in your barn pay schooling fees, while students can hire whomever they want to braid, let the customer know ahead of time. NO ONE LIKES FINANCIAL SURPRISES.

❖ Well in advance post dates of upcoming events that may interest your customers in a place where they will see it.

❖ Make your customers active participants in developing your business. Constantly ask them what you could do to make your business more to their liking.

❖ On a regular basis give your customers the unasked for, unexpected something extra.

> **For example:** You have a customer who has been boarding with you for 3 months and you have a lesson program. Put a free lesson coupon along with a note that tells them how much you appreciate their business in an envelope and either tack it to their stall door or give it to them in person. If you have a customer who hires your carriage, give them a coupon worth $5 or $10 towards their next carriage ride.

❖ Always talk to an unhappy customer as soon as you know they are unhappy. If you leave your ego out of it and sincerely try to solve the problem, you may not only save the customer; you may save your business. If a customer leaves unhappy, you loose more than their business, you loose the friends the customer could be sending to you.

Most businesses that fail do so because they don't communicate well with their customers.

The most common reason that people are unhappy with your services is a lack of communication. You either didn't clearly explain things at some point or they failed to tell you of a problem at a point when you could have addressed it to their satisfaction. It is important that your customers feel they can come to you with their problems and that you will listen and be willing to make changes. Occasionally you will have a chronic malcontent who is more destructive to your barn than the income they give you is worth. The only way to deal with this sort of person is to get them out of your barn as quickly as possible. However, good communications with the rest of your customers will keep the damage such a person can cause to a minimum.

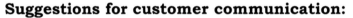

Communication isn't just about getting your messages out; Communication requires that you get information from your customers and employees as well. Really listen when anyone comes to you about anything to do with your business. They might be able to point out problems before they become big ones saving you lots of time and money.

Suggestions for customer communication:

❖ Brochures that give a general outline of what you offer.

❖ Price sheets and descriptions of services

❖ Bulletin boards for messages from you and your customers.

❖ Written policies that outline rules, customer obligations and services that are included for the price, and those for which there is an extra charge. Any changes in the policies must be given to the client in writing and posted in several locations.

❖ A newsletter published 2, 4, 6 or 12 times a year depending on the amount of information that interests your clients.

❖ Regularly scheduled meetings with your customers if the nature of your business allows for it.

❖ Make your customers and employees feel valued and that their efforts on your behalf are greatly appreciated. Everyone appreciates a pat on the back.

❖ Do your best to be approachable. When anyone comes to you with a problem, don't shoot the messenger. Be grateful that they are bringing the problem to you so that a solution can be found and bigger problems avoided.

Chapter Ten

The Marketing Plan

As I have said on many occasions, one of the most costly mistakes business owners and managers make is failing to have a firm marketing plan from the day they start their business. All too often, business owners and managers treat marketing as a fly-by-the-seat-of-you-pants operation. They have no idea what, when or where they are going to advertise, put together a brochure, or attempt to promote in the media. They simply open their businesses or launch new services and wait until an advertising sales person comes knocking on their door.

Without a marketing plan, they don't place advertising with outlets that they have researched and know for a fact reach their target market audience. They don't have a carefully planned time for ads to run when they will be most effective. Ultimately, they end up spending a lot of money on ads and other promotions that don't work.

If instead, they would take the time to put together a marketing plan before hand, they could eliminate a lot of unnecessary and costly "Let's try it" marketing and see much better results with far less stress and cost.

While the very name implies a lot of mysterious work, creating a marketing plan is not difficult. A marketing plan is simply putting down on paper your starting point, what your marketing goals are, who you want to respond to the marketing (the target market), what message you are going to focus on, how you plan to reach your goals, how much time your marketing efforts are going to take, how much you plan to spend, how you plan to spend it, and how you plan to measure your results

Your Starting Point

If you want to succeed with marketing, you have to know what your business is doing before you start. How many customers you presently have, how much they are paying for each service, what you are grossing each month, quarter or year and what the profit margins are will help you determine what you have to do to get where you want to go and keep you abreast of how close your are getting to your marketing goals and when you actually reach them. So take the time to go over your records to get an accurate picture of your business's financial picture.

What You Want to Accomplish

Creating an effective marketing plan requires that you determine what it is you want to accomplish. Do you want to start a new business, or launch a new service for an existing business? Do you want to increase your business (your annual income or profits)? How much of an increase can you realistically aim for? Do you want to increase your presence in the market place, improve name recognition, or generate more interest in what you do?

The Target Market

As with all marketing efforts, before you can plan an effective marketing campaign you must identify who your target market is so that you will know how to tailor your message and the medium you use to deliver that message. It is imperative that you identify this market if you want to increase your chances of success. Ask yourself exactly who is it that you want to obtain as customers; more of your existing market, or an additional market? Can you expand your market to include an additional group or should you develop a new service for your principle target market?

In other words, if you are working with advanced hunter seat riders, should you go after beginning or intermediate riders or should you try to develop a new service for advanced hunter seat riders such as attending more rated shows away from home, or hosting special clinics that focus on more advanced skills.

If you have an equine assisted psychotherapy business that services young girls with addiction problems, you might consider addressing additional problems that young girls encounter, developing a service for the parents of young girls with addiction problems or developing a new service for young males with addiction.

*Note: In most cases you are wiser to add services for existing customers (target market) than you are to go after an additional market that requires a very different marketing approach.

How You Are Going To Reach Your Goal

Once you have identified what it is you want to accomplish, you need to determine how you are going to reach that goal or goals. If you want to increase the size of your annual income, can you expect to get this increase from marketing your existing services or do you need to create a new service or product? Can you repackage your existing service to make it more appealing to additional markets? Can you expand the size of the area you are servicing; is it possible or realistic to market your services to people outside the area?

*Note: this option is more likely if you go to the client instead of them coming to you, or if you have, or have access to residential facilities such as bunkhouses, cabins or RV hookups.

When you have a clear idea of how you are going to go after a larger market or increase your markets, you need to decide on how best to reach them with your message. Are you going to rely on advertising, or public relations, or both? How much can you reasonably afford to spend?

Of course the other thing to consider at this point is what your benefit message is going to be. What customer need are you going to promise to address? What single Benefit about your service are you going to make the focus of your campaign? This benefit message will have more to do with your effectiveness than any other single element in your marketing plan.

Timing

When you set out to plan your marketing, you need to have a set time period. Are you going to launch a year long campaign, or one that lasts one month, two, a quarter of a year or more? Knowing the time allotted can help you determine whether you want to spend your entire budget on a blitz - placing ads in as many outlets as possible to run simultaneously such as for a special event, or if you need to pace your advertising, direct mail or other promotions so that they help to build longer-term results. Unless you have a major new service or new business that you are trying to launch, the wisest course is to develop campaigns that run for at least 6 months. This allows your target market the opportunity to get to know you and have your message imprinted on their brains in a manner that will build long-term relationships.

If all you can afford to spend is $25 a month, you can market your business.

Understanding your time constraints also makes planning for press coverage easier as most publications and television shows have special issues and programs that may be perfect for promoting your services. If you know when these special issues or programs occur **before** you develop your marketing plan, it is easier to schedule things so that you can best take advantage of such press or advertising opportunities.

Budget

There are no hard fast rules governing how much money you should spend on marketing. However, the general rule of thumb is that you should spend 5% of the total amount you want to bring in. The reality may be that you often don't have that much to spend. In the end, what matters most is not how much you budget, but how well you spend your marketing dollars. If all you can afford to spend is $25 a month, once you allocate that amount, you can then determine how to spend it in a manner that will get you the most bang for your buck. So don't worry about how much or how little you can afford, just put down a number and put together the rest of your marketing plan by deciding how you are going to spend it.

How You Are Spending Your Budget

Are you going to advertise? Where? How often during the campaign? If you are running a six month campaign, will you have enough money to advertise every week or month or will you have to advertise only on alternate months or weeks? Are you going to develop a brochure or other marketing materials? How much are they going to cost? When do you have to have them ready to distribute? How are you going to distribute them? What are the distribution costs? Are you going to attend any trade shows or consumer shows aimed at your target market? What marketing materials will you require for such shows and how much are they going to cost? Are you going to seek press coverage? Which media are you going to use and what are you going to try to get them to cover?

Without measuring results, you can't possibly get the most out of your marketing efforts.

Every one of these items needs to be considered as part of your marketing plan. Once you decide which items you plan to utilize, you need to write them down as part of your marketing plan. You may also find that it is helpful to also write down why you are choosing a particular action. It can be as simple as –"I am running an ad in this particular publication because it is where I get all of my information." Or "I am working on getting an article placed in this magazine because I feel that it reaches my target audience more effectively than any other publications I reviewed." Or "I chose to post flyers in tack shops because I believe that my potential customers are most likely to go there and trust information they find while there." Or "I am running this ad because their sales rep assures me that they reach my audience.

Writing down the reasons for your actions may seem unnecessary; after all you wouldn't do something if you didn't think you had a good reason for doing it. However, if you write down the reasons for your choices, you can later review your plan and see if your reasons were on target or overly influenced by your personal beliefs or a good sales pitch.

Measuring Results

It is amazing to me that many people will plan every aspect of their marketing except measuring their results. It is rather like going on a diet and never stepping on a scale. Of course you might be able to tell how successful the diet is by how lose your clothes become. But that too is just a means of determining results. But if you wear lose fitting clothes when you begin your diet and never get on a scale, how will you know if are succeeding, if the effort you put forth is actually reaping the desired results? If you don't know what is working, how do you decide if you should keep doing it or look for something else? The truth is without measuring results, you can't possibly get the most out of your marketing efforts, particularly if you plan to have more than one marketing campaign.

Make sure that you get the best results in the long run by deciding from the very beginning exactly how you are going to determine the results of your marketing efforts. The means of doing so are simple. You can set up a spiral note book with a copy of your ads or news article placing one on each page along with the dates it runs and any costs incurred. Every time the phone rings or someone drops by, always ask where they heard of you or what made them call. Record every call generated by the ad or article with a simple tick mark. If callers tell you what made them call you or what they liked best about your ad, brochure, etc, write it down in detail. Another method of gauging results of a marketing plan is to track your income during the months prior to the campaign and see how they compare with your income once the campaign has begun. You can also track the number of clients you had before you began your campaign, versus the number you have after you begin you marketing efforts. What ever means of tracking you decide to use is up to you, just make sure you have a reasonable, easy to use method of tracking and make certain that everyone in your business knows what to do and does their part. Tracking doesn't work unless everyone who answers the phone or interacts with clients is making the effort to discover how new clients are learning about you and what is making them choose you over the competition.

On pages xl-xliii in the Appendix you will find a blank form that you can use to develop your own marketing plan. There are also templates available with many word processing programs that can be used to make your marketing plan development easier. Feel free to use what ever works best and easiest for you.

Following are two sample marketing plans.

Marketing Plan 1:
XYZ Horse Business

Starting Point: We presently have 100 clients who pay us $145 an hour for at least one equine assisted therapy session per week. Our annual income is $225,000 which provides a profit of $45,000 or 20% of gross.

Goals: We want to increase our overall business by 20%. To reach this goal we are going to need to increase the number of client hours by attracting new clients and encouraging existing clients to schedule more sessions. We will need at least 20 new clients or a combination of new clients and additional sessions for existing clients that will equal 20 additional paid hours of service per week for a total revenue increase of $2900 a week or $145,000 per year. If we increase the business by more than 20 additional paid hours of service per week, we will have to hire one additional staff member at a cost of $40,000 per year in salary and benefits. This means we will then have to increase the number of clients even more to offset the additional cost of personnel so we want to limit the growth to 20% at this time.

Target Market: We specialize in working with adolescent girls 12-18 years of age from families with a combined income of $50,000 per year or more, so our campaign will be aimed at the mothers of these girls.

Benefit Message: We are going to emphasize the life benefits we offer including: Developing better self-esteem, decision making, self-discipline, leadership, cooperation and team work.

Timing: This marketing campaign will cover a 6 month period beginning June 1 and ending December 31.

Budget: $7250

Marketing Actions:

  Advertising –

Ad in Local Society magazine – three ¼ page ads to run June 1, August 1, and October 1.

Cost of Ad Space: ($575 per ad) $1725 total

Cost of Production: Artwork, copy writing and layout $350

Total Cost: $2075

Number of contacts: 65,000 circulation.

Cost per contact: $0.32

Why: This publication was chosen because their demographics indicate that 100% of their readership matches our target market.

Brochures – 1000 copies of 4 color – 3 panel brochure to be distributed via direct mail to existing client base and referrals, and via a dispenser placed in 4 area tack shops.

Cost of brochures: Artwork, copy writing and layout $650, printing $600 total cost $1250

Cost of Distribution: $.37 postage for 200 clients and referrals -$74; 4 dispensers @$8 each = $24: Total cost $98.

Cost per contact: $1.35

Why: We know that it is easier to get someone who has spent money with us in the past to do so again than it is to get new clients. This brochure will remind our existing and past client base of the value of what we do and encourage them to use our services again or increase the amount of services they are presently using. They will also have something to give to friends who may need our services.

Public Relations: Attempt to interest Society Magazine by letting them know that our client demographic is the same as the magazines therefore their readers will find what we do of great interest.

Cost: $0 **Run Time:** Ideally in July

Why: This magazine reaches our target market and because we are advertising with them they will be more inclined to run an article.

If the magazine does not respond – host a demonstration of what we do and invite the media. We will serve refreshments for the media. **Cost:** $200 for refreshments. **Cost per contact:** depends on the number of media that attend and their circulation or audience. **Run Time:** End of July

Why: By having a media event, we can increase the number of contacts and improve our name recognition.

Attempt to schedule and appearance on local talk radio program and local TV shows.

Cost: $0 **Run Time:** Ideally at least one show a month during campaign.

Why: These shows have a good local audience so being on them will increase public awareness and attract new customers.

Host a Charity event with profits to go to a charity that addresses the needs or interests of our clients such as a youth shelter or crises center. Send press releases to media.

Cost: While there will be some initial costs, participants will pay to attend event, there should be profits and therefore no costs to us. If we do not have enough paid participants we will have to absorb any losses. These can be reduced through sponsorships and by getting donations of ads and other promotional materials.

Run Time: In October.

Why: This event will attract the media and further increase public awareness of our business and attach it to a cause that is meaningful to our customers thereby creating a positive feeling about us.

Measuring Results/Tracking: We will ask every contact where they heard of us and record their answers. We will also track the number of new clients after each ad, event, article and brochure is distributed.

Pretty Cute Ponies Marketing Plan

Starting Point: We presently have 25 clients who pay us $45 an hour for at least one session per week. Our annual income is $56,250, which provides a net profit of $6,750 or 12% of gross.

Goals: We want to increase our overall business by 25%. To reach this goal we are going to need to increase the number of client hours by attracting new clients and encouraging existing clients to schedule more sessions. We will need at least seven new clients or a combination of new clients and additional sessions for existing clients that will equal seven additional paid hours of service per week for a total revenue increase of $175 a week or $8,750 per year. If we increase the business by more than seven additional paid hours of service per week, we will have to purchase two new horses at a cost of $8,000 plus upkeep of approximately $5000 per year. This means we will then have to increase the number of clients even more to offset the additional cost of ponies so we want to limit the growth to 25% at this time.

Target Market: We specialize in working with beginning western riders, primarily girls 6-12 years of age from families with a combined income of $40,000 per year or more, so our campaign will be aimed at both the girls and the mothers of these girls.

Benefit Message: We are going to emphasize the life benefits we offer including: Developing better self-esteem, decision making, responsibility, self-discipline, leadership, cooperation and team work.

Timing: This marketing plan will cover a 6 month period beginning June 1 and ending December 31.

Budget: $1,000

Marketing Actions:
    Advertising –
        1000 Flyers
            Cost of Production: Artwork, copy writing and layout $350; printing at Office Depot - $.05 each. Total $50

            Distribution: Post in local tack shops and feed stores, mail to area elementary and middle schools, day care centers and public libraries.

            Cost of Distribution: $0

            Total Cost: $50

            Number of contacts: 1000 **Cost per contact:** $0.05

            Run Time: Attempt to distribute a minimum of 200 flyers per month.

            Why: Flyers are a low cost means of making the public aware of what we do.

        Placemats – 1000 copies of the North American Horseman's Association's "Horse Facts" placemats that include my contact information.

            Cost of Placemats: 1,000 $88 including postage; stamp with contact information $25; Total cost- $113

Cost of Distribution: $0 **Cost per contact:** $.12 **Run Time:** Attempt to have restaurants use 150 placemats per month.

Why: Restaurants will use the placemats to entertain the kids while they wait for food. The colorful placemats will engage the children's interest and make them and their parents aware of our lesson and boarding program.

Tack Stall Curtains, photos and flyers – To use at all horse shows.

Cost: Curtains with our name and contact information $800, frames and photos of our riders $25, flyers $.05 each. **Cost per contact**: Depends on how many shows we attend and how many years the curtains last

Why: The tack stall curtains, photos and flyers will make us look more professional and experienced to those attending the horse shows increasing public awareness of our business and generating more interest.

Public Relations:

Attempt to interest Society Magazine by letting them know that our client demographic is the same as the magazines therefore their readers will find what we do of great interest.

Cost: $0 **Run Time:** Ideally in August issue when parents are looking for after school activities.

Why: This magazine reaches our target market and no one can resist a story about little girls and their horses.

Host a demonstration of what we do and invite the media and area families. We will serve refreshments (punch, cookies and chips) for 50 people.

Cost: $50 for refreshments.

Cost per contact: depends on the number of media that attend and their circulation or audience.

Run Time: A Saturday in September.

Why: By having a media event, we can increase improve our name recognition and increase interest in our services.

Attempt to schedule and appearance on local talk radio program and local TV shows.

Cost: $0

Run Time: Ideally at least one show a month during campaign.

Measuring Results/Tracking: We will ask every contact where they heard of us and record their answers. We will also track the number of new clients after each ad, event, article and brochure is distributed.

Chapter Eleven

What to Do When Your Marketing Efforts Work

So, you've followed my advice and the phone has started ringing and people are constantly dropping by. You should know by now that your marketing materials alone are not going to convince someone to buy your goods or services. Their only function is to get potential customers to you door or on your phone. After that it is up to you to do the rest, to "close" the deal.

Closing sales can be an involved and complex process but for most horse business owners it is a matter of reinforcing your benefit message and learning to ask questions. What are your riding goals? What are you looking for in a farrier? What do you consider to be the most important thing in a boarding facility? What kind of horse do you have? What is it you plan to use this horse for? These are all questions you probably ask instinctively. The key is to get the customer to sell himself or herself by asking questions that allow you to give answers that reinforce your benefit message and remove the negatives.

Eliminating Negatives

Early on in this book, we discussed the need for you to honestly evaluate your business's strengths and weaknesses. The strengths should already be part of promoting your business. The trick is to take the weaknesses, the negatives that make you less than perfect and make them work for you.

Before you can transform negatives into positives, you must first know what those negatives are, and how you can make them less important. Again, your benefit message, the thing about you that appeals most to potential customers' emotions can help you.

For example: I have a client who has a boarding facility that is about five miles farther out than other boarding barns in her area. The single biggest obstacle she faced in keeping her stalls full was that horse owners complained that it was inconvenient because

they had to drive an additional 5 to 10 minutes to get to her. I suggested that she address this issue head on by addressing the real issue – convenience - in her ads. The benefit message was "We are the Most Convenient Barn in Town." The copy for the ad read – *Convenience isn't just about driving distance. Convenience is quality service that keeps you from having to come out to the barn just to check on your horse. At XYZ stables we take such good care of our horses that their owners only show up when they want to ride. We do the work so that you can have all the fun.* The driving distance became a non-issue with most boarders and her stalls are now full.

Make a list of your negatives and create a plan on how to make them less important before you begin to promote your business. Make a list of what is important for clients to know about you and keep it near the phone. Take notes so that you will be able to use what a potential customer asks or complains about to improve your business and your presentation. Don't write a speech; just try to cover the high points in the course of the conversation. Keep it natural and most of all, sincere. And never forget to ask for the sale.

Make a list of your negatives and create a plan on how to make them less important before you begin to promote your business.

The More Information Trap

Recently one of my clients contacted me about changing her brochure and/or creating a follow-up packet of information. It seems that my client had received several calls in response to her ads and brochures. During the phone conversations several of these potential customers asked for "more information." Understandably my client thought that this meant she did not have enough information in her ad or original brochure, the one that generated the calls. Her solution was to add more information to the original brochure and create a packet of follow up information.

What my client failed to realize is that these potential customers weren't looking for more information; the callers were instead looking for a reason to buy her services. They were giving my client the opportunity to "sell" them on using her program instead of someone else's. In other words her original brochure had worked. She simply forgot the cardinal rule of marketing: *The purpose of ads and brochures is not to sell your goods or services. The purpose of ads and brochures is to stimulate interest so that potential customers will call or come to your place of business and give* **YOU the opportunity to sell your goods or services**.

What my client should have done in these situations was simple; ask what additional information the caller needed. Were they curious about her qualifications and training? Did they need to know how to go about scheduling a lesson or what types of lessons she offered? Did they want to know what they could expect during a lesson and what kind of progress they could expect? How did this progress rate relate to the caller's goals? And so on, and so forth.

Each one of these questions could have been answered over the phone in a manner that would have gotten the caller more interested in contracting for her services. Each is a selling point that should be used to convince the potential customer that her services are valuable, easy to obtain and better than the competition.   If the caller was unsure of exactly what more he needed to know, she could then have asked questions that would help her discover exactly what information he felt he still needed.

To be even more effective it is a good idea to jot down these questions and their answers on a sheet of paper while you are on the phone. After a few moments you will have a better idea of what exactly the caller needs to hear to make their decision. And don't forget to ask for the sale before the person hangs up. In such situations the best thing to do is ask – have I answered all of your questions? If so, then ask for the sale by saying, "I have some openings next week. What is better for you, morning or afternoon?" Then depending on their answer offer a suitable time on the first day available. It is important to note that when you reach this stage of the call you should not ask a question to which the caller may answer yes or no. What you ideally want to do is give the caller a choice between two things that are acceptable to you. In other words, don't ask if they want to set an appointment, instead ask what time or day is more convenient and give them two times or days that you have open. If you simply ask if they want to schedule an appointment, you are giving the opportunity to say "no." Once they do so, you have lost the sale and a potential customer.

*Avoid questions that can be answered with "yes" or "no." Give your clients a choice between two things, either of which is acceptable to **you.***

If the person still feels the need for more information once the call is completed, consider the sale lost. If you are feeling particularly stubborn, then use your notes to compose a letter restating your answers to the caller's questions, and your strongest selling points. 90% of the time such tactics do not work. The only time they do is when you are dealing with a caller who works for a large company that is looking at a group activity, and they have to sell their boss or bosses on the idea of using you. Occasionally you will also see this happen with a parent who has to run things by another parent. In such situations it is a good idea to use the information you gathered to get a feel for what it is the company or person is looking for, and how you can help them meet those goals. Then you can restate your benefits in a follow up letter. You may also learn that the company uses a bid process and what steps you need to take to make such a bid.

At the very least, never let a caller get away with asking you to send more information. You will never sell them by sending more brochures or paper because this is not what they really want. What they really want in such circumstances is help making a decision. It is up to you to make sure that their decision is to use you. Don't let the opportunity pass you by.

General Rules for Selling:

❖ Be friendly and sincere.

❖ Hit the high points of what you have to offer.

❖ Ask for the sale by offering the customer a choice between two things - would you like to take a lesson on Saturday at 1 or 4? Do you want the stall by the tack room or would you prefer the one by the door to the paddock? Do you want me to shoe on Tuesday or Friday?

❖ **NEVER SAY ANYTHING BAD ABOUT YOUR COMPETITION**. Even if they are the worst, most incompetent, dangerous, crazy people on earth. Even if the potential customer says bad things about your competition first. Even if the potential customer says great things about them. **NEVER, NEVER, NEVER, NEVER, NEVER SAY ANYTHING BAD ABOUT YOUR COMPETITION.** To do so makes you look bad. It sends the message that you talk about people behind their back. It makes you look worse than the competition.

Remove any potential for embarrassment by making what the customer is to do as clear as possible.

Winning Customers

People, all people, hate to feel stupid, or feel uncertain about how they are to proceed. People will avoid such situation for fear of embarrassment. Make sure that you remove any potential for embarrassment by making what the customer is to do as clear as possible.

Signs can be a big help in this area. Use them to mark the entrance to your facility. Label all the buildings and parking areas. If you have only one building and one parking area, make certain you have signs that point the way to your office or where ever you generally are.

When you are in the lesson ring, or barn, post a sign on your door saying where you are and what time you will be available or invite visitors to come to the ring to watch. Put a bench or bleachers at ringside if you have the room so that they will have a comfortable place to observe.

Always answer the phone as pleasantly as possible and make certain that your employees do the same. Always be courteous. Return calls and phone messages promptly. People who are calling you are looking to buy what you are selling. If you aren't available, or don't get back to them promptly, they are going to your competition.

While a potential customer is at your place of business or if they phone, try not to let them go without getting their contact information. Once you have this, send them a short hand written note thanking them for coming by or calling, and tell them how much you look forward to working with them or their child, or horse, or whatever. This is an incredibly effective way to "seal the deal." Who wouldn't want to board, or ride, or have their horses treated by someone who takes the time to give them such special notice.

Chapter Twelve
Building Customer Loyalty

I t is an absolute fact that it is cheaper and easier to get someone who spent money with you once to spend it with you again, than it is to go out and get new customers. This being the case it is surprising that businesses spend the majority of time and money on soliciting new customers and give no thought to how to keep the customers they already have and to increase the services they offer them. Once a customer is doing business with you, you should be working on increasing their loyalty to you and expanding the opportunities they have to spend money with you.

Successful trainers have long understood this concept, at least in principle. They move a customer beyond the lesson program by convincing them to buy a horse, which is then boarded at the trainer's stable. Once the horse is bought the next push is to get the student showing. Eventually, the customer is taking advantage of every service the trainer has to offer. This is ideally what every business owner should aim for and then some.

The optimum of all marketing is to have a customer not only taking advantage of every service you offer, but so loyal that they not only tell everyone about you, they bring you new customers. To move customers up to this level takes effort and understanding.

I have known some trainers who confuse loyalty with codependency. They keep customers by undermining the rider's self-confidence to the point that the rider is terrified to ride without the trainer by her side. These trainers are often verbally abusive, and the really dangerous ones are so subtle in undermining self-confidence that a casual observer would never notice. This approach requires a certain, megalomaniacal personality disorder that can be very destructive to all parties involved.

The truth is that you do not have to resort to such destructive techniques. The best way to build customer loyalty is to provide good service, communicate any changes well in advance, never hit your customers with unexpected financial surprises, be open to suggestions, resolve problems quickly, make sure that your customers feel that they can come to you and that when they do you will listen and do your best.

Ultimately, it is the small acts of courtesy that build loyalty and wins new customers.

Eddie Federwisch, the director of Equine Studies at Virginia Intermont College, is a whiz at this sort of thing. He goes out of his way to make everyone who attends a VI hosted show feel valued and appreciated. At intercollegiate shows, he gives buckets of lollypops to each team. At schooling shows he has special treats for exhibitors. They are always small, inexpensive things, but they are the unexpected, something extra that builds loyalty.

At the college's annual USEF rated show, the VI Classic, Eddie makes sure that every trainer has two VI students assigned to him or her for the duration of the show. These students serve as "show angels," who help unload horses, unwrap legs, setup feed and water buckets, and do anything else to help the trainer and they do it for free. If you ask anyone who has ever attended a VI show since Eddie has been in charge where their favorite place to show is, they will tell you VI. Even if they lost, they love to go back because they know that their presence is appreciated.

Creating the kind of work environment people enjoy working in is the foundation of any profit generating customer service program.

Keys to Profitable Customer Service

A lesson program is first, last and always a service, to make the most money you have to have profit generating customer service.

Profit generating customer service requires that you provide the kind of service that your existing customers value enough to want to continue paying for and that potential customers find valuable enough to want to come to you instead of your competition.

YOUR STAFF

Creating the kind of work environment people enjoy working in is the foundation of any profit generating customer service program. There are a large number of books written on keeping good employees, but they all boil down to a few basics, treat people as you yourself would like to be treated, pay fairly and on time, be quick to praise and slow to criticize, be realistic in your expectations, communicate clearly what you expect from people by having written job descriptions and don't ask people to do more than what is in those job descriptions. Most importantly make your staff aware that their attitudes and behavior towards clients has a significant impact on your business. Why? Customers do business with people, not businesses. Human beings establish relationships and are more likely to continue to do business with people they like and are comfortable around. If your staff is happy and feels that they are being treated fairly, the customers will pick up on this attitude. Your barn will be a pleasant place that riding students and their parents like to be. If your barn is filled with disgruntled workers, the atmosphere in the barn will reflect their displeasure and it won't be a place healthy, sane people want be.

Make sure that everyone in your barn is part of the customer service program. Establish a system for dealing with problems and make sure everyone knows what the system is, and their role within. Once you have a system in place, don't stick with it if it doesn't work. Be vigilant and willing to change when necessary.

YOUR COMPETITION

Any business can be successful if it offers something people want and has no competition. If you are the only reining barn in town you might be able to get away with substandard customer service, at least you will up until the day another reining barn opens in your area.

Most of you however, aren't the only game in town. Therefore customer service is a critical part of winning and keeping good customers. To do so, take a good objective look at what your competitors are doing to provide service for their customers. Do they keep the barn immaculately clean? Do they offer special services? Do they have lots of social activities? How do they communicate with their customers? Find out everything you can so that you can plan your own customer service program.

THE 80/20 RULE

In business you will find that you earn 80% of your income from 20% of your clients. Find out who your 20% are and look for new ways to improve service to them. Ask them what new services you can provide that will make their experience with you better. Is there any thing they think you can improve on?

UNDERSTAND VALUE

Customers are only wiling to pay for what they feel is valuable. Do you know how your customers determine value in a riding program? Generally speaking, most riding lessons are purchased by parents who know little or nothing about the horse industry. How did they choose you over other instructors in the area? Why do they continue to do business with you? Once you know what your customers value about your service, you should have a clear idea of what you should continue to do, improve upon and highlight in your advertising.

For example: If parents tell you they chose you because they felt you were more positive in your instruction than other trainers, you might want to put "Lessons with a Positive Approach," in your next advertising campaign.

AGGRESSIVELY SEEK COMPLAINTS

This does not mean you should corner a student or parent in a stall and tell them that you heard they were unhappy. What it does mean is that you should do is keep your eyes and ears open for unhappy customers and attempt to address their complaints as quickly as possible.

The reality of business is that customers don't come to you with complaints. Rather than tell you when something is wrong, they tend to just go elsewhere, rather than give you the opportunity to correct the problem. This happens most often because people are uncomfortable telling you of their problems or because they don't feel that it will change things for the better if they do. Make it clear to your customers from the very beginning that you are there to see that they are receiving the best service possible and that you want their help in identifying problems so that you can correct them.

Provide a means for people to tell bring problems to your attention in non-threatening, emotionally safe ways such as an anonymous suggestion box, regular barn meetings with customers where you set aside time to discuss complaints and separate meetings with employees to do the same.

Whenever a client tells you of a problem, treat it as if they are doing you a tremendous favor, which indeed they are. Pointing out problems gives you an opportunity to provide better customer service which retains existing clients and helps you attract new ones.

Your first priority should be finding a solution, not defending yourself or justifying whatever is at the root of the problem.

RESPOND

Once you learn of problems, respond as quickly as possible. Don't let complaints go unattended to or your customers will stop coming to you and resort to complaining to each other or other trainers or riders from other barns. Any time you are given the opportunity to uncover a problem, your first priority should be finding a solution, not defending yourself or justifying whatever is at the root of the problem.

Always be willing to admit when you are wrong and to change.

COMMUNICATE EFFECTIVELY

In most cases problems are the result of poor communication. Profitable customer service begins before the client takes the first lesson. It is wise to have a policy that all new students come to the barn at least 2 hours before their first lesson, or on a separate day. Take the time to give the client a complete tour of your facility. Provide a written list of barn policies, rules and procedures. Emphasize that you and the staff are there to handle any problems the client may have, but you first must know about the problems. Tell clients what your complaint procedure is, give them a copy of this procedure and follow the procedure you have written down. Make it as simple as possible so that clients and staff can easily comply. At the very minimum make a policy that anytime a staff member sees, hears or is brought a problem, that the staff member bring the complaint to you and that you write down the problem, who made the complaint, the day and time the complaint was made, what was done to address the complaint and what the end result was. Always take the time to follow up with the client to make sure the problem has been addressed to their satisfaction.

Right about now, you are probably rolling your eyes thinking you can't possibly do this because with the volume of bellyaching that goes on in your barn, you'd never get anything done. If that is the case then you need to take a serious look at the cause. Yes, it seems that horse people are demanding and have unrealistic expectations. However, proper communications can help clients to understand what is realistic and what is not.

COLLABORATE

A great way to improve service is to be able to partner with other businesses. Is the local tack shop willing to give your clients a 10% discount or offer free delivery to clients at your barn? Is there an area trainer that can take students further than you can? Are there local trainers who teach disciplines that you don't teach? Would they be willing to refer students interested in your style of riding if you refer students to them?

Take a good look at those local businesses that compliment what you are doing and see how they can help provide better service to your clients in a manner that will benefit all parties involved.

Ultimately, customer service is a state of mind. If you put the customer first, if you do your best to meet reasonable needs in a timely fashion, you will provide good customer service and have more clients than you can handle.

Chapter Twelve and a Half

Still Waiting for Your Prince?

My workshops, like this book, are aimed specifically at professionals in the horse industry who don't have lots of money to spend on marketing. I try to provide information specifically to help them build their businesses with the smallest budgets imaginable. Over the years, I have spent a lot of time and energy preaching about how to get free-publicity, and how to create effective low-cost advertising.

So it surprised me when I was going over evaluations after a workshop I conducted for a group of riding instructors. When I got to the end of one particular evaluation, the person had written "Great presenter, but ideas too lofty for my small business. Maybe someday."

I cannot tell you how much these wistful comments disturbed me. Firstly it was upsetting because I had not read these remarks until after everyone was gone and, therefore, could not address the issue head on. But mainly because it made me aware that there may be others who have attended my workshops or that will read this book and think the same thing. That is very unsettling to me because, if you think your business is too small to benefit from sound marketing practices that are absolutely attainable on even the smallest of budgets, then your business will NEVER be anything more than a small business, if you remain in business at all.

You now have a choice. You can either sit around hoping that someday your prince will come and rescue you from your lonely, unprofitable life, or you can take the information in this book and put it to work letting your prince know that you exist, and luring him to your door.

Don't put it off because you don't have the time, or the money. Make the time now. Decide how much you can afford – even if it is as little as $10 a week, if you invest it properly you can see results and begin to watch your business grow.

So quit putting things off until the day you make enough money to launch a huge, expensive campaign. Start doing small things now and it won't take long to get to the point where you can afford to spend a hundred times, a thousand times more than you can spend right now.

Marketing your business is a mind-set, not an economic obstacle. If you concentrate on what you can do, instead of how little money you have, you can see results. It doesn't cost you a thing to call your local civic organizations and get on their list of speakers. A small classified ad in a local paper can cost less than $25 a week, one in a local shopper publication can cost about the same or sometimes even less. If you own a computer, a flyer on the bulletin board at your local grocers will cost you nothing but your time, the ink and paper. So stop making excuses and start promoting yourself, NOW. If you don't, no one else is going to.

Take a lesson from Rapuntzel. Her prince didn't come until after she launched her low-cost marketing campaign, which consisted of good signage (her long flowing hair), and a well-sung, snappy tune that got his attention. So put up some flyers and start singing as loudly as you can. Not only will your prince come, you'll join the elite club of horse professionals who are making a very good living doing what they love.

Aim High and go for it!

Appendix

Despite the name, this is really important suff.

The forms that follow are copyrighted and may not be
reproduced without written consent.

Size and Composition of Your Potential Market

Name of the Location (nation, state, county, or city) you plan to sell your products or services to _____
_____

Size of the area in square miles: _____ (relevant if customers come to you or you go to them. Less important if you plan to do business via Internet or catalogue sales.)

Total Population of area: _____

Number of Females: under 8 yrs _____   8-14 _____   15-18 _____   18-29 _____   30-40 _____
45–55 _____   56 & up _____

Number of Males: under 8 yrs _____   8-14 _____   15-18 _____   18-29 _____   30-40 _____
45–55 _____   56 & up _____

Size of geographical area _____ sq. miles

Total Annual Household Income (the number of families in this geographical area that make each of these amounts)
Below $25,000   _____
$26,000 - $35,000   _____ $50,000 - $75,000   _____
$36,000 - $40,000   _____ $75,000 - $100,000 _____
$40,000 - $50,000   _____   Above $100,000   _____

Horses in this area -(information may be available through state dept of ag. or state horse council and breed associations)
Total Horse population is this geographical area _____ head
# of Quarter Horses _____   Thoroughbreds _____   Arabians _____
   Warm bloods _____   Saddle bred _____   Paints _____
   Draft _____   Appaloosa _____   Passo Finos _____
   Miniatures _____   (Add other breeds your business may require)

Riding styles and the number of people in the area for each -(information is available through the various riding associations and magazines aimed at each discipline)
_____ Western Pleasure   _____ Hunters
_____ Reining   _____ Jumpers
_____ Roping   _____ Dressage
_____ Cutting   _____ Driving
_____ Arabians   _____ Tennessee Walkers
_____ Quarter Horse Competitions   _____ Eventing
_____ Trail   _____ Therapeutic Riding

Distance from the largest concentration of this population to your place of business _____ miles (relevant if customers come to you or you go to them. Less important if you plan to do business via Internet or catalogue sales.)

Number of direct competitors that are between you and the largest concentration of your target market _____
(How many similar businesses are closer than you to the largest concentration of your target market?) See Appendix B for more information on competitors.

Number of the following in your market area:

Tack Shops _____   Farriers _____   Haulers _____

Boarding Facilities _____   Available Stalls _____   Show Facilities _____

Riding Instructors _____   Trainers _____   Equine Veterinarians _____

Equine Message Therapists _____   Equine Dentists _____   Equine Acupuncturists _____

Breeders* _____   Feed Stores _____   Horse Insurance Brokers _____
*(This may need to be broken down by each individual breed if your business focuses on a particular breed)

Number of Horse or Riding Specific Local Magazines or Tabloids _____

Number of Other Magazines or Papers Aimed at Your Target Market _____
Showing Opportunities in Your Discipline:

Number of shows requiring little travel from home per year: Schooling _____   Rated _____

Number of shows requiring you to travel more than one hour from home: Schooling _____   Rated _____

Number of colleges/schools that have IHSA /IDA/RIFNA/IEA or other riding team: Colleges _____   Middle/High schools _____

Number of colleges or schools that may be interested in sponsoring a riding team: Colleges _____   Middle/High schools _____

The Size and Composition of Potential
EAL Corporate Training Market

Name of the Location (nation, state, county, or city) you plan to sell your services to: _____
_____

Size of the area in square miles: _____

Total Population of Area: _____

    Number of Females: under 23-29 _____ 30-39_____ 40–55 _____ 56 & up _____

    Number of Males: under 23-29 _____ 30-39_____ 40–55 _____ 56 & up _____

Number of College Graduates in your Area (available through state education census) _____

Total Annual Household Income (the number of families in this geographical area that make each of these amounts)
Below $25,000 _____ $26,000 - $35,000 _____ $50,000 - $75,000 _____

$36,000 - $40,000 _____ $40,000 - $50,000 _____ $75,000 - $100,000 _____

Above $100,000_____

How many Businesses and Organizations in your area Employ (Available through area Chamber of Commerce or State Economic Census):

    10 or less _____   10-30 _____   31-60 _____   61-75 _____   76-100 _____

    101-200 _____   201-500 _____   Over 500 _____

How many Businesses or Organizations have Boards of Trustee who meet in your area: _____

Business and Community Service Organizations in your area:

Name	# of members in your area
_____	_____
_____	_____
_____	_____
_____	_____
_____	_____
_____	_____
_____	_____
_____	_____
_____	_____

Distance from the largest concentration of this population to your place of business _____ miles.

Number of direct competitors that are between you and the largest concentration of your target market _____
(How many similar businesses are closer than you to the largest concentration of your target market?) See Appendix B for more information on competitors.

Corporate Training Programs in your area - (information is available through the phone book and possibly the Chamber of Commerce)

_____ Team Building   _____ Communication   _____ Leadership Training

_____ Board Training   _____ Customer Service Training   _____ Problem Solving

_____ Life Coaching   _____ Conflict Resolution   _____ Mediation

The Size and Composition of Your Potential EAP Market

Name of the Location (nation, state, county, or city) you plan to sell your services to: _____
_____

Size of the area in square miles: _____

Total Population of Area: _____

    Number of Females: under 4-11 yrs _____   12-17 _____   18-29 _____   30-39_____

            40–55 _____   56 & up _____

    Number of Males: under 4-11 yrs _____   12-17 _____   18-29 _____   30-39_____

            40–55 _____   56 & up _____

Total Annual Household Income (the number of families in this geographical area that make each of these amounts)

    Below $25,000 _____ $26,000 - $35,000 _____ $50,000 - $75,000 _____

    $36,000 - $40,000_____ $40,000 - $50,000_____ $75,000 - $100,000 _____

    Above $100,000 _____

Distance from the largest concentration of this population to your place of business _____ miles.

Mental Health Disorders in your area the number of members for each - (information is available through the various national, state and local associations)

_____ Anorexia & Bulimia		_____ Substance Abuse	
_____ Obesity		_____ Juvenile Offenders	
_____ Attention Deficit/Hyperactive Disorder		_____ Victims of Sexual Abuse	
_____ Learning Disabilities		_____ Victims of Physical & Emotional Abuse	
_____ Autism/Asberger		_____ Sex Offenders	
_____ Grief		_____ Behavioral Disorders	
_____ Depression		_____ Emotional Disorders	

Number of the following in your market area:

LCSW _____	MSW _____	Psychiatrists _____
Psychologists _____	Therapists _____	Public M. H. Care Providers _____
Marriage Counselors _____	Family Counselors _____	Clergy _____
Educational Consultants _____	School Counselors _____	Guidance Counselors _____

School Administrators (Public & Private) _____

Private Residential Treatment Facilities _____	Capacity _____
State Residential Treatment Facilities _____	Capacity _____
Probation Officers (Juvenile) _____	Case Load _____
Probation Officers (Adult) _____	Case Load _____
Court System Administrators _____	Area Recidivism Rate _____

continued

Organizations that address the Primary disorder or condition you plan to address:

Name	# of members in your area
_____	_____
_____	_____
_____	_____
_____	_____
_____	_____

Number of the following who work with you target market

Counselors _____   Therapists _____   Psychologists _____

Psychiatrists _____   Treatment Programs _____   Residential Treatment Centers _____

Number of direct competitors that are between you and the largest concentration of your target market
_____ (How many similar businesses are closer than you to the largest concentration of your target market?) See Appendix B for more information on competitors.

Organizations that address the second disorder or condition you plan to address:

Name	# of members in your area
_____	_____
_____	_____
_____	_____
_____	_____
_____	_____

Number of the following who work with you second target market

Counselors _____   Therapists _____   Psychologists _____

Psychiatrists _____   Treatment Programs _____   Residential Treatment Centers _____

Number of direct competitors that are between you and the largest concentration of your target market
_____ (How many similar businesses are closer than you to the largest concentration of your target market?) See Appendix B for more information on competitors.

Sizing Up The Competition

In addition to other businesses that offer the exact same services as you do, there may be numerous businesses that offer seemingly different services that are still competitors. (Indirect competitors)

For example: You teach riding lessons to children ages 6 - 16. Not only do you need to know what other riding instructors are charging, it is a good idea to know what other sports lessons in your area cost. This information can be very helpful in setting your price and in defending this charge to any parents who question why riding lessons cost so much more than baseball or piano lessons.

On this form you should try to list as many comparable services offered as well as other potential competitors for your clients time and money. If you have more competitors than this form will hold make additional copies or write the information in a notebook.

Direct Competitors:

1. Name: _____ Location: _____

   Services Offered: _____ Fee per Service: _____

   Strengths: _____ Weaknesses: _____

2. Name: _____ Location: _____

   Services Offered: _____ Fee per Service: _____

   Strengths: _____ Weaknesses: _____

3. Name: _____ Location: _____

   Services Offered: _____ Fee per Service: _____

   Strengths: _____ Weaknesses: _____

4. Name: _____ Location: _____

   Services Offered: _____ Fee per Service: _____

   _____ _____

   _____ _____

   _____ _____

   Strengths: _____ Weaknesses: _____

   _____ _____

   _____ _____

   _____ _____

   _____ _____

   _____ _____

5. Name: _____ Location: _____

   Services Offered: _____ Fee per Service: _____

   _____ _____

   _____ _____

   _____ _____

   Strengths: _____ Weaknesses: _____

   _____ _____

   _____ _____

   _____ _____

   _____ _____

   _____ _____

6. Name: _____ Location: _____

   Services Offered: _____ Fee per Service: _____

   _____ _____

   _____ _____

   _____ _____

   Strengths: _____ Weaknesses: _____

   _____ _____

   _____ _____

   _____ _____

   _____ _____

   _____ _____

Indirect Competitors

1. Name: _____ Location: _____

   Services Offered: _____ Fee per Service: _____

2. Name: _____ Location: _____

   Services Offered: _____ Fee per Service: _____

3. Name: _____ Location: _____

   Services Offered: _____ Fee per Service: _____

4. Name: _____ Location: _____

   Services Offered: _____ Fee per Service: _____

5. Name: _____ Location: _____

   Services Offered: _____ Fee per Service: _____

Vision: How You See Yourself Determines How the Customer Sees You.

Fill in the blanks below to help better define your vision of yourself.
Don't be shy or embarrassed by what you write. This is the time to dream big.

"We _____."
(How are you different from your competitors?)

"To be the _____ of _____."
(Whom do you want to emulate?)

"Helping people _____."
(What do you do for your customers?)

"It's about _____
_____."
(What are you about?)

"Preeminent _____."
(What contest do you want to win?)

"_____ means _____."
(What is the essence of your business?"

"Famous for _____."
(What are/do you want to be famous for?)

Tip: many of these statements can become the basis of future advertising. Use them as a slogan along with your logo at the bottom of printed ads or at the end of radio or television ads.

GOALS: Where Is Your Business Headed?

Goals may include things such as the number of students, customers or horses you want to have, the number of horse shows or trail rides you would like to attend or conduct, how much you want to increase your revenues, etc.

This year I will:

1.) _____

2.) _____

3.) _____

4.) _____

5.) _____

In 3 years I will:

1.) _____

2.) _____

3.) _____

4.) _____

5.) _____

In 5 years I will:

1.) _____

2.) _____

3.) _____

4.) _____

5.) _____

Tip: Long-range goals are not set in concrete. They can and should be changed as competition,

Identifying Your Product or Service
What is it that you are selling?

Most people in the horse industry don't understand that they are selling a product. Aside from horses most of what is sold in the horse industry is less tangible; i.e. lessons, training, board, etc.

Using the information that you itemized in Pricing Part II - Determining your income to fill in the spaces below to help form a better idea of what you are "selling."

List the top 5 income generators for your horse business; i.e. group lessons, private lessons, group trail rides, custom trail rides, partial board, full board etc. You will need to determine not only which ones bring in the most revenue but also which ones are generating the greatest percentage of profit.

For example: Full board may bring in $45,000 per year, but when you subtract the cost of supplying board - property, insurance, stable hands, water, utilities, feed and hay, farm equipment, etc. you may find that you are actually loosing money or that you are realizing a profit of only 5% of your total board cost. On the other hand you may discover that while your group lesson program generates only $20,000 a year your cost for supplying instruction for riders on their own horses is such that you are realizing a profit percentage of 55% or better. In such a case you would list your group lesson program as the first product you are "selling".

Your most popular products based on profit percentages:

1. _____ which realizes _____% annual profit

2. _____ which realizes _____% annual profit

3. _____ which realizes _____% annual profit

4. _____ which realizes _____% annual profit

5. _____ which realizes _____% annual profit

This should give you a better idea of what it is you are actually selling. However the key to selling more is to understand what it is your customer is "buying."

Sample Customer Survey

(This sample survey is for riding instructors but can be adapted for any business. To create your own survey questions should be designed to provide an accurate picture of the age, sex and buying habits of your customers.)

The information below should provide you with a clear profile of your largest customer group, including age, sex, lesson and show habits and horse purchases. Verify your information by checking your records and those of your employees. Do not guess!

1. How many lessons do you teach each month? _____

2. How many of your students take:
   1 lesson per week _____   2 lessons per week _____   3+ lessons per week _____

3. How many of your students are female aged: (If a students takes more than one lesson per month count them as an additional student. For example if you have a student aged 17 who takes 3 lesson per week you need to count that student as 3, not 1.)
   5-7 _____   8-10 _____   10-12 _____   12-14 _____   16-18 _____   18-20_____

   21-25 _____   25 - 30 _____   30 - 40 _____   40+ _____

4. How many of your students are male aged: (If a students takes more than one lesson per month count them as an additional student. For example if you have a student aged 17 who takes 3 lesson per week you need to count that student as 3, not 1.)

   5-7 _____   8-10 _____   10-12 _____   12-14 _____   16-18 _____   18-20_____

   21-25 _____   25 - 30 _____   30 - 40 _____   40+ _____

5. According to age, how many of your female students attend classes during the week?

   5-7 _____   8-10 _____   10-12 _____   12-14 _____   16-18 _____   18-20_____

   21-25 _____   25 - 30 _____   30 - 40 _____   40+ _____

6. According to age, how many of your male students attend lessons during the week?

   5-7 _____   8-10 _____   10-12 _____   12-14 _____   16-18 _____   18-20_____

   21-25 _____   25 - 30 _____   30 - 40 _____   40+ _____

7. According to age, how many of your female students attend classes during the weekend?

   5-7 _____   8-10 _____   10-12 _____   12-14 _____   16-18 _____   18-20_____

   21-25 _____   25 - 30 _____   30 - 40 _____   40+ _____

8. According to age, how many of your male students attend classes during the weekend?

   5-7 _____   8-10 _____   10-12 _____   12-14 _____   16-18 _____   18-20_____

   21-25 _____   25 - 30 _____   30 - 40 _____   40+ _____

continued

Riding Instructor Survey continued

9. According to age, how many of your female students are beginners?

5-7 _____   8-10 _____   10-12 _____   12-14 _____   16-18 _____   18-20 _____

21-25 _____   25 - 30 _____   30 - 40 _____   40+ _____

Intermediate -

5-7 _____   8-10 _____   10-12 _____   12-14 _____   16-18 _____   18-20 _____

21-25 _____   25 - 30 _____   30 - 40 _____   40+ _____

Advanced -

5-7 _____   8-10 _____   10-12 _____   12-14 _____   16-18 _____   18-20 _____

21-25 _____   25 - 30 _____   30 - 40 _____   40+ _____

10. According to age, how many of your male students are beginners?

5-7 _____   8-10 _____   10-12 _____   12-14 _____   16-18 _____   18-20 _____

21-25 _____   25 - 30 _____   30 - 40 _____   40+ _____

Intermediate -

5-7 _____   8-10 _____   10-12 _____   12-14 _____   16-18 _____   18-20 _____

21-25 _____   25 - 30 _____   30 - 40 _____   40+ _____

Advanced -

5-7 _____   8-10 _____   10-12 _____   12-14 _____   16-18 _____   18-20 _____

21-25 _____   25 - 30 _____   30 - 40 _____   40+ _____

11. How many rated shows/rodeos/trials do you attend each year? _____

12. How many schooling shows/rodeos/trials do you attend each year? _____

13. According to age, how many of your female students attend rated shows/rodeos/trials each year?

5-7 _____   8-10 _____   10-12 _____   12-14 _____   16-18 _____   18-20 _____

21-25 _____   25 - 30 _____   30 - 40 _____   40+ _____

14. According to age, how many of your male students attend rated shows/rodeos/trials each year?

5-7 _____   8-10 _____   10-12 _____   12-14 _____   16-18 _____   18-20 _____

21-25 _____   25 - 30 _____   30 - 40 _____   40+ _____

continued

15. What divisions do your students compete in? (Please list division and number of each student who participates in that division over a one-year period.) Example- <u>Short Stirrup- 6</u>

_____   _____   _____

_____   _____   _____

_____   _____   _____

_____   _____   _____

_____   _____   _____

16. What additional services do you provide at shows/rodeos/trails? And how many students pay for each of these services:

Grooming ___   horse hauling ____   leg wrapping ____   schooling student____

Schooling horse ____   horse day-care _____   transporting of tack box ____

_____ _____

    (Other -specify)

17. How many moms stay at the barn for the full lesson time? _____

18. How many dads stay at the barn for the full lesson time? _____

19. How many grandparents stay at the barn for the full lesson time? _____

20. How many of your students under 18 are dropped off and picked up at lessons? _____

21. How many moms attend horse shows for students 18 and under? _____

22. How many dads attend horse shows for students 18 and under? _____

23. How many grandparents attend horse shows for students 18 and under? _____

24. How many of your students under 18 are dropped off and picked up at shows? _____

25. What are the income levels of your students' and their families?
(List the number of students who are in each category)

    $40,000 or below _____ $61,000 - 75,000 _____

    $40,000 - 50,000 _____ $76,000 - 100,000 _____

    $51,000 - 60,000 _____   above $100,000 _____

Pricing: Part I - Determining Your Costs

How much do you pay each year for:

Property - rent, lease or 1st or 2nd mortgage	$_____
Property Taxes - including school and other tax	
levied on your property	_____
Property Insurance	_____
Business Insurance	_____
Marketing	_____
Legal Fees	_____
Feed -	_____
Hay -	_____
Water -	_____
Utilities - Electricity and/or gas or heating oil	_____
Salaries - including your own	_____
Employee Benefits -	_____
Professional services - accountant, attorney, etc.	_____
Veterinary services -	_____
Farrier services -	_____
Horses - purchases or leases	_____
Tack - purchases and repairs	_____
Trailer - loan payments and/or upkeep	_____
Truck - loan payments and/or upkeep	_____
Tractor and other farm equipment - payments and/or upkeep	_____
Gasoline for trucks and other farm equipment	_____
Barn, fences and pasture maintenance	_____
Professional Development- classes, conferences and	_____
Workshops that enhance your ability to do your job.	
Horse Transport - any paid shipping for horses	_____
Personnel Transportation - for you and/or employees	_____
Total annual costs	$_____

Pricing: Part II - Determining Your Income

How much do you make and where does it come from?

Trail Rides - Group $_____

Trail rides - Custom   _____

Horse Sales   _____

Horse Purchases for client   _____

Lessons - Group   _____

Lessons - Private   _____

Board - Partial   _____

Board - Full   _____

Pasturing -   _____

Training   _____

Horse Show Schooling   _____

Horse Shows - Host or presenter   _____

Horse Hauling   _____

Judging   _____

Clinics   _____

Lecturing   _____

Shoeing   _____

Grooming   _____

Health Care Services - de-worming, injections, message   _____
            Wound or injury care, other special treatments

Other (specify) _____   _____

Total annual income $ _____

Pricing: Part III - Determining Your Present Profit Margin

Total annual income (determined in part II) $ _____

Total annual expenses (determined in part I)   Subtract   _____

Total annual profit or loss (income less expenses) $ _____

Percent of annual profit over expenses (profit margin)*   _____ %

*To determine profit percentage, divide the total expense by the total profit -

For example: if you have a total annual expense of $39,000 with an annual profit of $5,000
Divide $5,000 into $39,000, which equals 7.8 %.

Identifying Your Audience

Creating any successful promotional piece begins with determining the person you are trying to reach with your message. There is always a temptation to create promotional pieces that are aimed at the largest variety of people. This is a mistake. The key to success in marketing is to focus on a single well-defined group – the kind of person most likely to be interested in and willing to spend money on your services. **For example:** *if your greatest success is in teaching students who want to compete nationally, then you need to focus your brochure on the parents of such riders.* It won't do you any good to mention that you also teach adults who ride as a hobby. If you do teach these adults and you want to build this portion of your business as well, then you will need to do a second brochure to promote it. The surest way to have ANY marketing piece fail is to try to make it promote too many things at one time.

When you focus on promoting just those services that appeal to one particular group, you can better determine appropriate colors, the kind of artwork, the sophistication of the language in the copy, the most suitable font, and most importantly the benefits to emphasize.

To help you identify your audience start by determining the service you wish to focus on. Choose either the largest existing area of your business or the area you want to build.

Most of my business consists of (or I have noticed a growing need for or interest in ?): _____

_____

_____

_____

_____

The type of person I teach (or want to teach) the most is: (identify gender, age, race, economic status, etc. Note: the more detailed you are, the better.)

_____

_____

_____

_____

_____

_____

Benefits Your Business Offers Potential Clients

Whether you are composing an ad, flyer or brochure, the key to a successful promotional piece is identifying and promoting the key benefits you offer. The piece must tell the clients – What's in it for them! What's in it for them! What's in it for them!

To help you get started simply list at least 10 benefits you offer clients. Remember to look at the benefits from your client's point of view.

You should come to us (or bring your child to us) because:

1. _____

2. _____

3. _____

4. _____

5. _____

6. _____

7. _____

8. _____

9. _____

10. _____

The Three Most Meaningful, Exciting and/or Fun Reasons For Doing Business With YOU!

While we would all like to believe that everything in life, all-important decisions, are made on sound rational reasoning and for a higher noble purpose, this is not the case. Human beings make decisions based on emotional reasons. If you key into the real emotional reasons a person may want what you have to offer, the more likely you are to sell them on coming to you. So take a good look at your list of 10 benefits and see if you can find three that appeal to the emotions.

For example: *if you have a good record for teaching beginning riders, you would emphasize that your build foundations that help kids become winners in life as well as the show ring. This approach appeals to the parent's emotional need to feel that they are doing everything they can to help their child succeed.*

Below please list the three benefits you offer that have the strongest emotional connection or appeal and what the emotion is that you are appealing to:

Benefit 1 _____

Emotion 1 _____

Benefit 2 _____

Emotion 2 _____

Benefit 3 _____

Emotion 3 _____

Your Most Important Benefit and Where to Use It

Of the three reasons with the strongest emotional appeal, which one is the strongest? Which one appeals to the most basic human need? Why?

The strongest emotional benefit I offer is: _____

_____

_____

Potential customers are most likely to find this to be my strongest benefit because

_____

_____

_____

When you have narrowed your benefits down to the most meaningful, you have the message that should be on the cover of your brochure. (You can also use this as the headline and message of any advertising you may do.) Note: *Always check your competition to see what benefit they are focusing on to promote their business(es). If they are using the same benefit, you may want to look again at your benefits to find a different one to focus on. Or you may need to find a way to tell your message differently while appealing to the same emotion.*

Your Brochure Cover

Let's take the most important benefit you have discovered in Planner #4 and use it to create the perfect cover for your brochure. To begin, look at your benefit. Now let's find a way to make to tell your audience about your benefit in the simplest most meaningful way. At this point, the simpler the language, the shorter the message, the better. Remember that we are trying to titillate and create interest so that anyone seeing the brochure cover will want to pick it up and look inside. It should be exciting and have impact with as few words as possible. The message can be in the form of a statement or question, but it must create interest. The K-I-S-S (Keep-It-Simple-Stupid) formula works best here.

Example: If you work well with kids who are more advanced, your message might be - *Tired of Being Stuck in the Same Place?* or *Wish You Could Do More?* or We *Can Take You to the Next Level* or *Reach for the Sky with XYZ Farms.*

My cover message is: _____

_____

_____

_____

Take this message and write it in on the Cover Panel of your brochure layout - **Brochure Planner**

Inside Your Brochure - Panel 1

Now that you have your main message, and a clear idea of the identity of the audience you are trying to reach it is time to move on to the inside of your brochure. The key here is to remember who your audience is and what will most appeal to them. We know what our main message is going to be; now we simply have to find the fastest and clearest way to get that message across. The whole point of a brochure is to create interest so that potential clients will call or come to your business so that you can sell them on your business. A brochure is not meant to tell the customer everything about you and your business. You don't have to go into great detail about how you do what you do. Remember the client cares most about results (benefits) and far less about how you get the results.

Inside the brochure you simply need to expand on your cover message. When doing so you can go back to your list of benefits and add 3-5 benefits with simple explanations of them. (See sample brochures). Remember to make it personal by using second person. "You can reach new heights…" Is more personal and meaningful than "One can reach new heights..."

The message I want to appear on Inside Panel #1 is –

_____

_____

_____

_____

_____

_____

_____

_____

_____

(See if you can simplify and/or shorten the wording before you transfer this information to Inside Panel #1 on your Brochure Layout form.)

Inside Your Brochure - Panels 2 & 3

If you need the space to continue to tell the exciting message of what benefits can clients receive by coming to you, do so on Inside Panels #2 & #3. Or you may need to divide your benefits into several parts, in which case you may do so on these panels. *It is a good idea to headline these sections with the strongest benefit you are trying to present.* **However it is also important to find space to include quotes from satisfied customers.**

Headline: _____

_____

_____

_____

_____

_____

Headline: _____

_____

_____

_____

_____

(If you need more room, feel free to write on the back of this page. Again, see if you can simplify or shorten the message before transferring it to your layout form. If you write too much, no one will read it.)

You and Your Qualifications

You may feel the need to include your qualifications. Do so only if you present your qualifications in a way that is meaningful to the client. Remember you are not trying to impress your peers (Unless of course you are selling your services to other riding instructors. If you are, then, by all means, include all the things that will matter to them.) **For Example**: Most people choosing a riding instructor have no idea what makes a good instructor but will want to know what makes you uniquely qualified to help them. If you have a college degree in an equine related field, they will want to know what you have your degree in. If you graduated from a college well known to clients, or well respected in your field then, include that too. Clients will also want to know if you are certified and by whom. Remember however that they will not care about anything that they do not understand. DO NOT USE ACRONYMS. Initials mean nothing to the layperson. ARIA means nothing to the average person– American Riding Instructor Association does.

Keep your bio short and sweet. Remember the idea is to create interest not tell your whole life story. Outside of academia, NO ONE reads a curriculum vita, NO ONE. If you don't have quotes from customers yet, then you need to give more information about yourself. If you have even a few quotes, you can tell less about yourself. If you have to choose between including your bio, or using quotes from customers – use the quotes. Nothing sells like happy customers.

I am uniquely qualified to provide the services I am selling because I am:

1. _____

2. _____

3. _____

4. _____

5. _____

Brochure Layout Guide Back

Outside Panel #1—Cover
Your Greatest Benefit Goes here!

Outside Panel #3

Your name and address go here if
this is a self-mailer.

Outside Panel # 2—
This is a great place for customer quotes

Brochure Layout Guide Front

Inside Panel # 3

HEADLINE

COPY

BIO

Call to Action

Phone Number

Inside Panel # 2

HEADLINE

COPY

HEADLINE

COPY

Inside Panel #1

HEADLINE

COPY

Sample of 3 Single Panel Brochure Fronts

laid out on a single page (it has been reduced to fit this space.) Once they are printed, they are cut to give you 3 individual brochures, each aimed at a separate market.

Sample of 3 Single Panel Brochure Backs

This is the other side of 3 single panel brochures laid out on the opposite page. Once printed they will be cut into three individual brochures and given to their specific market. Can you tell who the 3 markets are?

RIFNA MAKES IT POSSIBLE

These days even public schools have to worry about keeping their student numbers up. Competition for those students is fierce and admissions counselors and administrators need every tool they can get. According to several national horse organizations, there are hundreds of thousands of young riders across the US.

Riders Interscholastic Federation of North America makes it possible for you to attract these riders with an affordable club sport team. We also work with the schools to meet the requirements for RIFNA riders to letter in their club sport.

RIFNA MAKES IT AFFORDABLE

Our member barns provide the horses, tack, facilities, practices and shows including regular barn meets, area tournaments, state, regional and national championships at rates far below traditional lessons and shows.

QUALIFY FOR COLLEGE TEAMS & ATHLETIC SCHOLARSHIPS

There are 300 colleges participating in Intercollegiate Horse Show Association, 36 in Intercollegiate Dressage Association and 36 in NCAA sanctioned equestrian sports. Many of these colleges, including Ivy League schools, offer scholarships to qualified riders. RIFNA follows the same formats as the college programs. Our riders have an edge qualifying for teams and scholarships that help save the students money, and improve your overall scholarship numbers.

Sponsoring a RIFNA team for hunter seat equitation, dressage, western or all three can make a huge difference in your recruiting and retention efforts.

JOIN US!

RIFNA
Riders Interscholastic Federation of North America
SCHOLARSHIP   HORSEMANSHIP   SPORTSMANSHIP
770 781 3833
17875 BIRMINGHAM HIGHWAY
ALPHARETTA, GA 30004

RIFNA MAKES IT POSSIBLE

Riders Interscholastic Federation of North America makes it possible for you to attract more riders to your barn for team practices and meets as individuals or member of a school or barn team.

COMPETITIONS

If you have worked as a riding instructor or barn manager for any length of time, you know that shows are where the real profits are. RIFNA meets are short and easy so you can have more of them, more often.

RIFNA HELPS

RIFNA provides you the format, assistance in pricing, help with getting school recognition and support, suggestions for fund raising, as well as state, regional, and national competitions that give you and your riders the opportunity to show your skills, while making money for you and your business.

We also offer clinics and training to help you improve your skills, and special group rates on liability and other farm insurance.

JOIN US!

RIFNA
Riders Interscholastic Federation of North America
SCHOLARSHIP   HORSEMANSHIP   SPORTSMANSHIP
770 781 3833
17875 BIRMINGHAM HIGHWAY
ALPHARETTA, GA 30004

PURSUE YOUR PASSION

Riders Interscholastic Federation of North America makes it possible for you to ride Hunter Seat Equitation, Dressage or Western more often in regular barn meets, area tournaments, state, regional and national championships, as an individual or member of your school or barn team.

SAVE MONEY

RIFNA riders do not have to own a horse or tack. The barns provide the horses for practices and competitions. Our show fees are less expensive than traditional Shows.

QUALIFY FOR COLLEGE TEAMS

Because RIFNA competitions and rules follow those of the Intercollegiate Horse Show Association (IHSA) and the Intercollegiate Dressage Association (IDA), our riders are more familiar with the requirements and better able to rider unfamiliar horses selected in a draw and having your points count towards your team's overall score.

ATHLETIC SCHOLARSHIPS

There are 300 colleges participating in IHSA, 36 in IDA and 36 in NCAA riding programs. Many of these colleges, including Ivy League schools, offer scholarships to qualified riders.

FUN

RIFNA competitions and practices are fun because you are a member of a team, sharing your passion with people just like you.

JOIN US!

RIFNA
Riders Interscholastic Federation of North America
SCHOLARSHIP   HORSEMANSHIP   SPORTSMANSHIP
770 781 3833
17875 BIRMINGHAM HIGHWAY
ALPHARETTA, GA 30004

Want Your Horse Business to Succeed?

Everything you need to succeed in the Horse Industry.

The Horse Business ASSOCIATION

Membership Application

To join, visit www.horsebusinessassociation.com or fill out the form below and mail along with payment to:
The Horse Business Association, 6202 Stowers Rd., Dahlonega, GA 30533

Name: _____

Title: _____

Business Name: _____

Type of Business: _____

Number of horses in your care: _____

Number of students you instruct: _____

Address: _____

City: _____ Zip: _____

State: _____

Phone: (home) _____

(work) _____

(cell) _____

Email: _____

Website: _____

Type of Membership:
☐ Professional-$150 ☐ Individual-$45 ☐ Student-$15

Method of Pay- ☐ ment: ☐ Check (Pay to: Horse Business Association)

Credit Card: ☐ Master- ☐ Card ☐ Visa ☐ Discover
Am. Express

Credit Card Number: _____

Expiration Date: _____

Name on Card: _____

Signature: _____

Referred by: _____

So do we!

Any business associated with horses is time consuming, physically demanding and traditionally low profit. These simple facts prompted several professionals from different parts of the horse industry to come together to make things better for everyone.

It is our goal to use the expertise of our founders and members to help one another build more profitable and efficient horse businesses by providing you with everything you need to become more successful with less effort.

Who Can Benefit:

Show Facilities
Lesson Programs
Trainers
Carriage Services
EAP Programs
Colleges and Universities
Veterinarians
Associations & Clubs
Manufacturers
Artists
Massage Therapists
Students

Boarding Facilities
Riding Instructors
Breeders
Therapeutic Programs
Schools
Farrier's
Tack Shops
Publishers
Photographers
Haulers
Specialists
Appraisers

Anyone Who Works in or Services the Horse Industry

Benefits of Membership Include:

Professional/Business/School Membership - $150 annually

- Access to and affiliation with the largest network of knowledgeable professionals who actually make their living in the horse industry and will represent you and your interests, and help you improve your horse business.

- Access to experts who can provide the services you need at a special HBA discounted rate.

- Access to the discussion boards where you can ask for help, find information you need or just to get ideas that will make your life easier and more productive.

- Networking with other members

- Discount rates for advertising in newsletter and on the web site.

- Posting of contact information on the web site

- Quarterly newsletter filled with articles designed to make your job easier and more profitable - including tips on marketing, employee management, nutrition, pasture management, manure management, bedding, footing, insurance, accounting, liability and risk reduction, the latest developments in the industry and proposed legislation affecting the horse industry.

- Advance notice of special workshops and seminars designed to make your business more profitable.

- Advance notice of books, videos and other industry tools that can make a real difference.

Student Membership - $15.00 annually

- Access to the discussion boards where you can ask for help, find information you need or just to get ideas that will make your life easier and more productive.

- Quarterly newsletter filled with articles designed to make your job easier and more profitable - including tips on marketing, employee management, nutrition, pasture management, manure management, bedding, footing, insurance, accounting, liability and risk reduction, the latest developments in the industry and proposed legislation affecting the horse industry.

Individual Membership - $45.00 annually

- Access to experts who can provide the services you need at a special HBA discounted rate.

- Access to the discussion boards where you can ask for help, find information you need or just to get ideas that will make your life easier and more productive.

- Quarterly newsletter filled with articles designed to make your job easier and more profitable - including tips on marketing, employee management, manure management, bedding, footing, insurance, accounting, liability and risk reduction, the latest developments in the industry and proposed legislation affecting the horse industry.

Join Us Today!

Toll Free: 866.729.6268

www.horsebusinessassociation.com

The Horse Business ASSOCIATION

6202 Stowers Road
Dahlonega, Georgia   30533

Everything you need to succeed in the Horse Industry.

e-mail: info@horsebusinessassociation.com

Sample Logos

These sample logos demonstrate the different appeal you can get just by changing the fonts. Which do you find more masculine? Which do you find more feminine?

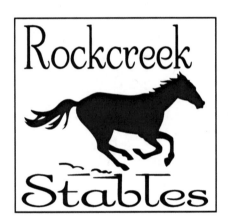 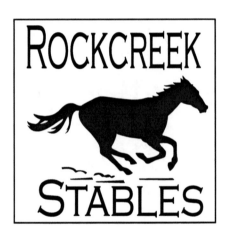

Sample Logos

These logos help to demonstrate how to change the art work and fonts to aim at different target markets.

Can you identify the logo aimed at western riders? Children? Which logos look they belong to a fun barn?

Which logos look like they belong to a barn that is more for serious competitors?

Sample Logos

Logos for Horse Businesses

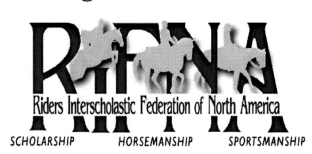

Because the market for the VIC Classic Horeshow is diffetent from the market for their equine studies program, this logo was created to give the show its own identity. The Equine Studies Program has another logo. We used two different logos to keep from confusing our two different markets.

Logos for EAP/EAL Businesses

*Note: To avoid confusing your clients, stay away from horse images

These two logos focus on the outcome that clients hope to achieve, not how they are going to achieve it. If you put a horse in an EAP logo, clients are more likely to think that you offer riding lessons.

The top Benefit your business offers YOUR CUSTOMER (what's in it for them!)

A brief statement that supports your benefit

Your Phone number

Your logo & company name

Teenager Driving you Crazy?

(000) 555-0000

You can have a Happier Family!

(000) 555-0000

EQUINE SERVICES, INC

Strategies for Winning the Game of Life!

We can help you build:
- A better Family
- A more profitable Business
- A better way of life

(000) 555-0000

EQUINE SERVICES, INC

Strategies for Winning the Game of Life!

PO Box 000   *   Santaquin , Utah 00000

A Better Team = Higher Profit$

(000) 555-0000

A Better Team = Better Profit$

(000) 555-0000

EQUINE SERVICES, INC

Strategies for Winning the Game of Life!

You can have a Happier Family!

(000) 555-0000

Ad Layout Sheet

A good basic layout includes your emotional benefit and phone number. If you have a logo or artwork and the room you can ad it.

22 word classified

1/4 page

1/8 page

1/2 page horizontal

Business Card Sample

HORSE SENSE

Experts in the Valuation of Hunter/Jumpers

The front of the card is reserved for contact information.

deSaix T. Hill

Certified EquAppraiser

American Society of Equine Appraisers

Phone: 337.943.1944

Email:desaixt@yahoo.com

181 Kenneth Boagni Sr. Drive
Opelousas, Louisiana 70570

To make the most of the card, the back is used to list the benefits of the service and the person's qualifications.

- **Know the true value of a horse before you buy.**
- **Sell your horse for what it is really worth.**
- **Get the appropriate insurance coverage.**
- **Legally validate you horse's value for legal and insurance claims.**

B. A. Equine Studies
Virginia Intermont College

Certified Level III
Hunter Seat/Equitation Instructor,
American Riding Instructor Association

20+yrs. Riding & Showing

Starling
Counseling for Women
HELPING YOU SUCCEED IN A CHALLENGING WORLD

Kim Starling, MA, EAP Level I   Office: (970)203-9995

email: kimstarling@mesanetworks.net

5131 S. College, Suite B   Fort Collins, Colorado 88525

Again we are using the front of the card for contact information and the back to list the benefits the potential customer will receive.

Providing you with the tools you need to:
- Face Life's Most Serious Challenges
- Conquer Your Fears
- Form Stronger Relationships
- Come to Terms with Loss
- Find Direction
- Get What You Need
- Revive Your Spirit
- Thrive

Sample Postcards

Postcards can be a low cost way to promote your business as long as you don't try to promote more than one thing to one market at a time. The card on the left is aimed at lawyers, the one on the right is aimed at horse buyers. There are several computer programs and papers to create postcards. You don't have to have an envelope and post cards cost less to mail. (These cards have been reduced to fit the space. You need to check with the post office to determine acceptable sizes.)

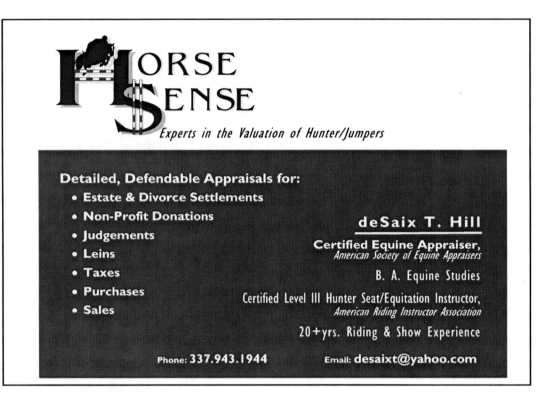

The Riding Academy of Acadiana llc

"I will not ride with common spirits."
William Shakespeare

Contact Us

Navigation:
- Home
- About Us
- Lesson Program
- Middle, High School & College Teams
- Acadiana Hunter/ Jumper Association
- Horse Board
- Medical Board
- Training
- Scouts
- Home Schoolers
- Calendar of Events
- Contact Us

- Reach Your Maximum Potential in the Arena and in Life
- Develop Riding Skills
- Find Your Horse's Magic Buttons
- Pursue Your Passion
- Live Your Dream

If you want to have lots of fun while developing and improving your riding skills, the Riding Academy of Acadiana is for you.

While we offer a variety of boarding and lesson options, we specialize in helping you to realize your dreams. Whether you want to learn to ride for your own enjoyment, or are in search of national championships, we have what you are looking for.

At the Riding Academy of Acadiana, horses are treated with respect and understanding. There are no quick fixes or harsh training methods. We use time and skill to overcome communication problems by tapping into each horse's unique personality. We train riders not passengers, because riders understand how to work with the horse and this understanding helps to develop skills that are used both on the horse and in life.

At the Riding Academy of Acadiana, riding is not a sport, it is our passion.

Billboard Layout Work Sheet

The chief benefit in 8 words or less

Logo or Name

PHONE NUMBER

A Gymkhana, Yippee!

Prizes! Fun! Kids! horses!

A day of Games on Horse Back for individuals and barn teams

* Games of speed

* Games of skill

* And much, much more designed to challenge horses and riders of all levels.

* Bring your horse, your parents and <u>your ASTM/SEI Certified Helmet</u>

WARNING: *Under Louisiana Law, a farm animal activity sponsor or farm animal professional is not liable for an injury to or the death of a participant in a farm animal activity resulting from the inherent risks of the farm animal activity, pursuant to R.S. 9:2795.1*

Riding Academy of Acadiana
Opelousas, Louisiana
Saturday, May 31, 2000
Games start at 9:00 a.m.

337-662-3920

Sample Student Press Release Form

Please type this over with the necessary information and mail to the sports or features editor of your local paper, or city magazines. (Make sure the contact person is the one who can answer any question on what is contained in the release in case the media calls for more information.)

Contact: Trainer or writer's name
Business Name
000 000-0000

For Immediate Release Please!

LOCAL RIDER PLACES ___ IN _____ (IDENTIFY THE COMPETITION)

_____ (student's full name) a student at _____

_____ (school) placed _____ out of _____ riders in the _____

_____ (division) at the _____ (event). _____

_____ (student's first name) rode to victory on _____ (horse's name), a

_____ (description of horse i.e. a chestnut colored large

pony. _____ (student's first name) has been riding since the age of _____ . She is

presently training at Ravenwood Stables with Janet Talmadge. This is _____

(student's first name) _____ (first, sixth tenth or whatever) show.

Note: If the competition is large enough or important enough and the student wins the event, it is a good idea to have this information together but instead of sending it in, call the features editor of your local paper and let them know just how important the win is and what a great human interest story it would be for their readers. If you do a good job of convincing them, they should ask to interview you and the students along with the family if it is a young child or if the family is well known.

Attach the actual ad, flyer or brochure to a notebook page and include the information indicated below. Then every time the phone rings or someone new comes by, ask where they heard of you. If they mention this show or prize list ad, put a tick mark in the appropriate space.

Full page ad in XYZ Farms Show Prize list
Run Date: July 2 (mail date) - August 21 (date of show)   **Cost:** $50
Distribution: Mailing out 300 copies and handing out about 100 more in tack shops.
Tracking period: July 2 - September 1.

Phone Calls: **Personal Visits:**

New Clients generated:

Marketing Plan Form

Marketing Plan

Starting Point: _____

_____

_____

_____

Goals: _____

_____

_____

_____

_____

_____

_____

Target Market: _____

_____

_____

_____

Benefit Message: _____

_____

_____

_____

Timing: _____

_____

_____

Budget: _____

Marketing Actions:
  Advertising – 1._____

  <u>**Cost of Production:**</u> _____

  _____

  <u>**Distribution:**</u> _____

  _____

  _____

  <u>**Cost of Distribution:**</u> _____
  <u>**Total Cost:**</u> _____
  <u>**Number of contacts:**</u> _____   <u>**Cost per contact**</u>: _____

  <u>**Why:**</u> _____

  _____

  _____

  2. _____

  <u>**Cost of Production:**</u> _____

  _____

  <u>**Distribution:**</u> _____

  _____

  _____

  <u>**Cost of Distribution:**</u> _____
  <u>**Total Cost:**</u> _____
  <u>**Number of contacts:**</u> _____   <u>**Cost per contact**</u>: _____

  <u>**Why:**</u> _____

  _____

  _____

  3. _____

  <u>**Cost of Production:**</u> _____

  _____

  <u>**Distribution:**</u> _____

  _____

  _____

Cost of Distribution: _____
Total Cost: _____
Number of contacts: _____   **Cost per contact**: _____
Why: _____

_____

_____

4. _____

Cost of Production: _____

_____

Distribution: _____

_____

_____

Cost of Distribution: _____
Total Cost: _____
Number of contacts: _____   **Cost per contact**: _____
Why: _____

_____

_____

Public Relations:
1. _____

Cost of Production: _____

_____

Distribution: _____

_____

_____

Cost of Distribution: _____
Total Cost: _____
Number of contacts: _____   **Cost per contact**: _____
Why: _____

_____

_____

2. _____

Cost of Production: _____

_____

Distribution: _____

_____

_____

Cost of Distribution: _____

Total Cost: _____

Number of contacts: _____   **Cost per contact**: _____

Why: _____

_____

_____

3. _____

Cost of Production: _____

_____

Distribution: _____

_____

_____

Cost of Distribution: _____

Total Cost: _____

Number of contacts: _____   **Cost per contact**: _____

Why: _____

_____

_____

Measuring Results/Tracking: _____

_____

_____

_____

_____

Additional Resources

Statistical Resources

<u>Trade, Breed and Discipline Associations such as:</u>
- American Quarter Horse Association
- US Equestrian Federation
- American Paint Horse Association
- American Appaloosa Association
- Arabian Association
- Carriage Operators Association
- Thoroughbred Association
- United States Dressage Federation
- United States Eventing Association

<u>Horse Councils</u>
- United State Horse Council
- State Horse Councils

<u>Government Agencies</u>
- Local and State Department of Economic Development
- US Department of Agriculture
- State Department of Agriculture
- County Agents

<u>Others</u>
- Local Chamber of Commerce
- University Departments of Agriculture-Agri-business & Agri-Economics
- Local Farm Bureaus

<u>For Equine Assisted Psychotherapists:</u>

Equine Assisted Growth and Learning Association (EAGALA)- The people who started equine assisted psychotherapy and the best training/certification program

National Mental Health Association (NMHA) www.nmha.org - This site has listings of almost every mental health care-related association.

Business Management

Small Business Administration (SBA) - http://www.sba.gov/
Women Business Owners - http://www.onlinewbc.gov/

Facility Planning

Horse Farm Planning - http://stablewise.com

Horse Fencing Guide Article -http://www.equisearch.com/horses_care/farm_ranch/fencing/fenceguide_101003/index.html

Public Relations Resources

North American Horseman's Association (NAHA) placemats with horse facts and horse activities that can include your contact information. Great to place in local restaurants that cater to families. NAHA, P.O. Box 223, Paynesville, MN 56362, www.arkagency-naha.com, 800-328-8894

The Publicity Hound's Tips of the Week Web site with lots of tips on how to get publicity. Published by Joan Stewart who has a lot of experience working with the media.   http://www.PublicityHound.com

Suggested Reading

Business Plan:
Plan for Profitability!: How to Write a Strategic Business Plan by Lee E. Hargrave; Paperback, 300pp Four Seasons Publishers: February 1999 ISBN: 1891929194

The One Page Business Plan: Start with a Vision, Build a Company! by Jim T. Horan, Tom Peters (Editor), Ruthie Petty (Illustrator): Paperback, 98pp: December 1998; The One Page Business Plan Company ISBN: 1891315072

Business Planner and Bookkeeper for the Horse Enterprise by Sue Ellen Marder, With Julia Flint; Paperback, 176pp; Breakthrough Publications, Inc. NY; May 1996 ISBN: 0914327658

Finance:
The SBA Loan a Step-By-Step Guide by Patrick D. O'Hara

Where's The Money by Art Beroff; Paperback:358 pages (May 1999) Entrepreneur Media Inc; ISBN: 1891984039

Where to Go When the Bank Says No: Alternatives for Financing Your Business by David R. Evanson Hardcover;256 pages Bloomberg Publishing ISBN: 1576600173

Marketing:
Positioning: The Battle for Your Mind - by Ries, Jack Trout / Mass Market Paperback / Published 1993 Reissue edition (February 1993) Warner Books; ISBN: 0446347949

The 22 Immutable Laws of Marketing: Violate Them at Your Own Risk by Al Ries, Jack Trout (Contributor) / Paperback / Published 1994 Paperback:160 pages (May 1994) Harperbusiness; ISBN: 0887306667

Graphic Design:
Creating Brochures & Booklets (Graphic Design Basics) by Val Adkins/Hardcover/ Published 1994 North Light Books; ISBN: 0891345175

Creating Logos & Letterheads (Graphic Design Basics) by Jennifer Place/ Hardcover/Published 1995 North Light Books; ISBN: 089134571X

The Non-Designers Design Book Robin Design and Typographic Principles for the Visual Novice by Robin Williams/ Paperback/Published 1994 Peachpit Press; ISBN1-56609-159-4

Advertising:
 How to Get Big Results from a Small Advertising Budget (The Learning Series) by Cynthia S. Smith Paperback - 194 pages Reprint edition (October 1995) Citadel Pr; ISBN: 0806516925

Public Relations:

<u>101 Ways to Promote Yourself</u> by Raleigh Pinskey Paperback - 393 pages (July 1997) Avon; ISBN: 0380785080

<u>Writing Effective News Releases: How to Get Free Publicity for Yourself, Your Business, or Your Organization</u> by <u>Catherine V. McIntyre</u> (June 1992) Piccadilly Books; ISBN: 0941599191

Horse Show Management:

<u>Hunter Horse Shows: Management A to Z</u> by Judy H. Spitzer, Spitzer Show Management

Available through: Judy H. Spitzer, Rt. Box 103, Verona VA 24482

Safety:

<u>Teaching Safe Horsemanship: A Guide to English & Western Instruction (Second Edition 2003)</u>

by Jan Dawson, President, American Association for Horsemanship Safety

154 pages, **available in most book stores or**

order from AAHS, PO Box 39, Fentress, TX 78622 for $19.95 plus $2 shipping

<u>Secure Seat: The Art of Staying on Your Horse and Learning Feel (2004)</u>

by Jan Dawson with Carole Chiles Fuller, 58 pages

order from AAHS, PO Box 39, Fentress, TX 78622 for $15.95 plus $2 Shipping

Helmet Facts: http://www.riding-instructor.com/helmets.php

<u>Liability and Risk Reduction Resources</u>

Insurance:

Always check with your horse association first before buying insurance for yourself and your facility. Often, these policies are the most affordable

Books:

> ***Equine Law and Horse Sense***, Julie I. Fershtman

> ***More Equine Law and Horse Sense***, Julie I. Fershtman
> Available through most book sellers or directly from the publisher

<u>State Laws Governing Horses, Horse and Facility Owners</u>

State Laws from American Association for Horsemanship Safety

> <u>http://www.law.utexas.edu/dawson/</u>
> An incredibly useful web site that has all the latest laws in each state (Statutes for Horsemen) in a downloadable format, Law cases for horsemen and articles on equine law as well as safety articles and the latest information from American Medical Equestrian Association.
> Web site created by Professor Robert O. Dawson, Bryant Smith Chair in Law, University of Texas School of Law. Site is funded by the University of Texas Law School and the American Association for Horsemanship Safety (AAHS)

Safety Issues

The American Association for Horsemanship Safety (AAHS)-Publishes a monthly newsletter that is packed with the latest in liability and safety issues http://www.horsemanshipsafety.com/

The American Medical Equine Association-Tracks statistics on horse related injuries with the goal of improving safety throughout the horse world. http://www.law.utexas.edu/dawson/amea/amea.htm

Risk Reduction Plans

The North American Horsemen's Association (NAHA) – Publishes a book with forms necessary to create your own risk reduction plan and includes sample contracts. The book is updated annually to keep abreast of changes in state and national laws. NAHA, P.O. Box 223, Paynesville, MN 56362, www.arkagency-naha.com, 800-328-8894